Jephthah's Daughter

A Tale of Obedience

BOOKS BY JOSEPH KENNEDY

Onesimus: Flight to Paradise
Lois: the Beauty of Holiness
The Invalid Warrior: Life of Paul
Chained to His Chariot: the Faithful Warrior
The Latter Years: the Ageless Warrior
From Eden to Canaan I: How the World Came to be the Way it is
From Eden to Canaan II: How the World Came to be the way it is
Epistle to the Hebrews
The Charm of Creation
Reverie: Poems to Ponder
Knigt of the Hourglass
The Beauty and the Bus

Jephthah's Daughter

A Tale of Obedience

Joseph Kennedy
Thee, Alabaster Box
Southside, Alabama

We would like to hear from you. Please write to us at any address below with your comments. We will reply. Thank you.

Thee, Alabaster Box
2106 Keenum Drive
Southside, Alabama 35907

Phone: 256 442 1466

Email: josephk6@charter.net

Web page: JosephsAlabasterBox.com

Jephthah's Daughter: a Tale of Obedience

Requests for information will be answered.

Dedication

For Cheryl Cornutt, librarian and lover of books,
Who loved this story, and encouraged me.

Jephthah's Daughter

and other selected short subjects

Joseph Kennedy

Original cover of this booklet

INTRODUCTION
to

JEPHTHAH'S DAUGHTER

an allegory based on

JUDGES CHAPTER ELEVEN

I have been intrigued by this difficult passage of Scripture for many years. I have consulted commentaries in search of a sound explanation of what happened to Jephthah's daughter. I have found little help, though some commentaries say that there are scholars who believe what I believe to be the true account. I cannot recall hearing a sermon preached from this text in the more than seventy years I have listened to preachers. (Since writing this, I heard Pastor Jeff Miss of Beth Haven Baptist Church, Crossville, Alabama preach an excellent message on this text.)

The problem of whether or not Jephthah actually sacrificed his daughter is one which most preachers and scholars find too far down their list of priorities to address. I address it because it is in the Word of God, and because most other subjects in the Bible are well covered by others. I do not claim any particular perception or revelation, but I do understand the English language quite well, and I am not afraid to read the Word of God literally.

This allegory was written to demonstrate the blessedness of a child who honors his or her parents even when the parents make foolish mistakes, and the blessedness of a man who is able to face up to his responsibilities to his word; and to God Who does all things well. The story illustrates the truth that a man should speak carefully and with prayerful thought; and when he speaks he should be absolutely bound by his word.

Jephthah's daughter was blessed because she was a devoted thing. A devoted thing must have a special place in the heart of God. A devoted thing would receive a special welcome in Heaven. Leviticus 27:28,29 says, "***Notwithstanding no devoted thing, that a man shall devote unto the LORD of all that he hath, both of man and beast, and of the*** *field of His possession, shall be sold or redeemed: every devoted thing is most holy unto the LORD. None devoted, which shall be devoted of men, shall be redeemed; but shall surely be put to death.*"

Those words are so clear and plain that they cannot be misunderstood. However, they can be ignored. We read that with horror because we think of death as a monster to be feared and dreaded. It is that, I do not deny, but it is also a gateway to the presence of God. The only way I can go to Heaven is to die or be raptured. I do not want to die today because I want to be with my family. But I understand that "*For me to live is Christ, and to die is gain.*" In the case of a devoted thing, to die must be to gain enormously. As a devoted thing, Jephthah's daughter gained more than the LORD has been pleased to reveal to us. My only question about what I believe about this incident is whether the girl was actually a devoted thing.

One objection that I have had to my interpretation to this story is that burnt offerings were killed, skinned, and burned. But Abraham did not do that to Isaac when he offered him in obedience to God's command in Genesis 22. Abraham was about to kill his bound son on the altar. It has also been said to me that only male offerings were made, but that overlooks the red heifer which was a female.

In remembrance of her, the Jews did not celebrate her death, but her virginity. Note that Judges 11:39, 40 says, "*... And it was a custom in Israel, [That] the daughters of Israel went yearly to lament the daughter of Jephthah the Gelidity four days in a year.*" Of course, they would not bewail her death because her death was a glorious victory of faith over the failures of the flesh. Her death was the obedience of a man so great he is recorded as a hero of the faith. They bewailed her virginity because for a woman to die without leaving children was a sad thing

Prologue

We are blessed by the privilege of living in the age of grace. We cannot imagine the inconvenience and frustration of living under the Law – the Law which was fulfilled by Jesus Christ. "... ***Christ hath redeemed us from the curse of the law, being made a curse for us: for it is written, Cursed is every one that hangeth on a tree:*** ..." says Galatians 3:13. We abuse our liberties, and consider not that we should live in liberty with great self discipline, obeying the commands of the Bible, especially those found in the New Testament.

Jephthah and the ancients did not enjoy such enormous blessings as we. Imagine committing a sin, and not having the privilege of going into the Holiest of all and pleading I John 1:9. Think of Achan whose sin resulted in his immediate death along with his family and all he owned. Others died for picking up sticks on the Sabbath. God had to punish the lawbreaker because the Substitute had not died. What a strain to live under the Law! Consider this, all you who would be justified by your own works.

Today we are so saturated with grace by the precious Word of God that we shrink back in horror from the thought of a man offering his own daughter as a burnt offering. But Jephthah was not guilty of murder as this little story will reveal. But we must conclude that Jephthah did honor his vow if we accept the Bible exactly as it is written, for it says, " ... ***at the end of two months, she returned to her father, who did with her according to his vow which he had vowed*** ..."(Judges 11:39).

This reveals the enormous power of the life and work of Jesus Christ Who delivered us from the curse of the Law. In three short years of ministry, and His death, burial, and resurrection, Jesus changed a people who had lived for fifteen centuries under a system of unyielding Law strictly enforced, to the sort of people we see in the New Testament who were called "Saints," and the church today. In three years, Christ made a total change in the religious beliefs and practices of Israel, and virtually the whole world. The Apostle Paul is a stunning example of this great power to change. He was instantly changed from a perfect example of law to a perfect example of Grace. Jephthah and his family lived under the burden of the Law, yet their faith in God's grace is an example that must encourage and motivate us today.

Judges 11:30-40

Judges 11:30 *"And Jephthah vowed a vow unto the LORD, and said, If thou shalt without fail deliver the children of Ammon into mine hands,*
31 *"Then it shall be, that whatsoever cometh forth of the doors of my house to meet me, when I return in peace from the children of Ammon, shall surely be the LORD's, and I will offer it up for a burnt offering.*
32 *"So Jephthah passed over unto the children of Ammon to fight against them; and the LORD delivered them into his hands.*
33 *"And he smote them from Aroer, even till thou come to Minnith, even twenty cities, and unto the plain of the vineyards, with a very great slaughter. Thus the children of Ammon were subdued before the children of Israel.*
34 *"And Jephthah came to Mizpeh unto his house, and, behold, his daughter came out to meet him with timbrels and with dances: and she was his only child; beside her he had neither son nor daughter.*
35 *"And it came to pass, when he saw her, that he rent his clothes, and said, Alas, my daughter! thou hast brought me very low, and thou art one of them that trouble me: for I have opened my mouth unto the LORD, and I cannot go back.*
36 *"And she said unto him, My father, if thou hast opened thy mouth unto the* LORD, *do to me according to that which hath proceeded out of thy mouth; forasmuch as the* LORD *hath taken vengeance for thee of thine enemies, even of the children of Ammon.*
37 *"And she said unto her father, Let this thing be done for me: let me alone two months, that I may go up and down upon the mountains, and bewail my virginity, I and my fellows.*
38 *"And he said, Go. And he sent her away for two months: and she went with her companions, and bewailed her virginity upon the mountains.*
39 *"And it came to pass at the end of two months, that she returned unto her father, who did with her according to his vow which he had vowed: and she knew no man. And it was a custom in Israel,*
40 *"That the daughters of Israel went yearly to lamentthe daughter of Jephthah the Gileadite four days in a year."*

AN ALTAR OF UNCUT STONES
DRAWN BY LESLIE NICHOLE KENNEDY

JEPHTHAH'S DAUGHTER

Jephthah watched his brothers play tag in the yard of their home in Gilead, and longed to play with them, but they would not allow him near them. He had grown accustomed to their savage treatment of him, that is, as much as a child can become accustomed to rejection by his family. He used to cry all the time, tagging after them, and begging to be included in one of the teams, but they pelted him with stones and curses. They hated him because his mother was not their mother. Jephthah had been born to a lewd woman in a nearby village, and his brothers did not consider him a brother. They were younger than he was, but he was only one against several, and they always prevailed when clashes occurred, which was often. Jephthah had to bear the reproach of his father's sin.

As the years passed, Jephthah became more bitter toward his family, and his rage caused him to become more violent. He began to run with violent boys. Then one morning he found his bed surrounded by his brothers, all armed with clubs, and scowls on their faces.

"You will leave this house for you shall not inherit in our father's house; for you are the son of a strange woman," said the brother who was the oldest of the group. His voice had a menacing tone, and Jephthah knew the boys would beat him to death if he tried to resist. Slowly, he got out of his bed, and dressed himself while his brothers' hostile eyes kept him fixed. He gathered up some of his personal things, and turned to them.

"I am my father's first born. I am his heir. I will return in due time to claim my inheritance, and I will return with a sword, and I will not come alone." At sixteen, he was tall and endowed with muscles.

"You will inherit nothing. You are not fit to be a member of this house. You will go and never return, or we will be prepared to meet you." Like a lion the voice came from deep in the chest through clinched teeth..

Jephthah shoved a boy out of his way and walked to the gate where he turned and looked at the group following him.. The brothers stopped at the gate and watched Jephthah walk sadly away from his home. He didn't look back. After he was out of sight they gleefully shook each others' hands, slapped backs, and offered congratulations all around.

Jephthah fled to Tob, which is Syria, and there he became a laborer in the fields. As he labored in the harvest, he saw a young woman he admired. He watched her, and tried to get close to her; but she seemed to want to be alone. He dreamed of her at night, and longed to know her, but what could it lead to? He had nothing to offer a wife. Yet, he was so stricken by her that even in the synagogue he could think of nothing else. Her face was before him day and night. When he could tolerate his feelings no more he watch her sit down as they ate their bread at noon. He sat down a distance from her, but near enough to her to speak to her. She paid him no mind.

"What is your name?"

"Leave me alone," she snapped.

Jephthah was stunned by the violence of her reply. For days it went through his mind like a flaming arrow. He continued to sit as close to her as he dared. He managed to gather courage to speak to her again a few days later:

"Why can't we be friends?"

"Why should we be?"

At least he could say another thing to her. "Because I have no friend, and you don't seem to have one, either."

"I am an unclean woman." The words were saturated with bitterness.

"I am an unclean man."

The girl looked at him, and Jephthah wondered if he were correct that there was a plea in the look.

As the harvest time wore on, Jephthah sat a little closed to the girl each day, longing to know her. One day she volunteered, "I am called by Tamar."

Her voice sounded like music, rich and clear, and the name was like a heartbeat to Jephthah. He was thankful for the words of the girl, and he treasured the memory as he gazed at the stars at night. Even in his dreams he could hear the sound of water bubbling over stones. Their next meeting found Jephthah sitting closer to her. She could hardly speak as she told him:

"My brothers forced me. They are older than me. They are men of belial. They gave my father a false story about me. My father made me leave my home." Her voice faded into tears.

Jephthah sat silently. Three days later, he sat near to her, and said, "Will you be my wife?"

"I am not meet to be a wife," she retorted.

Jephthah told the girl about his own life. He told her that he planned to go into the wilderness to live alone. At the end of the harvest, she consented to become his life partner. After their wedding, they went into the mountains, and began their lives. They had only a tent and some bedding, but they loved each other, and clung together as people having no family or friends in the world. They lost themselves so completely it was almost like living in Eden. Soon they were joined by another family who was wandering half-starved in the great wilderness. Jephthah hurried to the trap in the stream, and took out some fish. Tamar busied herself to prepare them. She had enough skins on hand to make the newcomers a small tent and some bedding.

The man told Jephthah that he had just been released from prison. He didn't want to live among people who despised him. He had no way of making a living, and didn't want to, anyway. Other men joined them as Jephthah's reputation spread. Some men had families. One man had lost a fortune, and was so angry that he wanted only to inflict death and injury to others. Simon had been rejected by a girl he loved, and wanted to avoid all his old friends. All the men who came had two thing in common: their lives were empty, and they admired Jephthah, and would give him their last drop of blood.

"Nadab! Why are you in bed when the sun is high?" Jephthah gave the sleeper a swift kick in the ribs. "Did I not command you to go north in search of meat?"

The man scrambled around in his bed, trying to get his senses together. He could think of no excuse as Jephthah threatened to strike him in the face.

"You will do your share of work, Nadab, if you are to remain in this company. Do you understand?" Jephthah was furious.

"All right. Jephthah," the man replied while he jerked on his mantle. "You should not come into my tent."

"I came in here with your wife's permission. She's as sick of your slovenliness as I am. Neither one of us will tolerate it any longer. Get you bow, and don't come back without meat."

Jephthah's anger rose no more as he watched the man disappear into a thicket, but he stayed angry all day. He was weary of the attitude of the whole camp. The men were not only irresponsible, but they had no skills in hunting and fishing. The men were poor hunters, and it was difficult to keep the band in meat. The wives were just as bad. Often he had to threaten them to force them to take baskets in hand, and search for berries and roots. He resolved then and there that he would make them into decent people, or he would take his family and leave. He told them of his decision that night around the fire.

A crisis arose shortly afterward that would impress everybody in the camp that they had better change themselves. The sixty men set up a new camp in sight of a small village. Before they were finished with the set-up of their tents, a group of armed men from the village confronted them.

"You must move from this place," the leader demanded. "We will not have you in our territory stealing and killing our sheep."

Jephthah pushed his way through his men, and faced the villager. "We do not steal or trouble anyone. We will stay here, and you need not be concerned about our presence."

"You will leave at once or we will come at you with sword and spear," the man insisted.

"Come at us with sword and spear at your own peril. We do not move easily. We will be prepared for your coming."

The man turned and strode away with his companions looking over their shoulders angrily.

Jephthah turned to his band, and said, "Shammaha, you take a man and watch first. Adino, you and a friend watch the south. Eleazar, you take a man and watch the east, and Dodo, you and a man go to the west and watch. I will assign others to relieve you. We mustn't allow these people to come upon us unnoticed. Has every man his sword sharp? Everyone not on duty get rest. The God of Israel will protect us from these heathen."

Through the night the men watched as a wispy fog covered the land. The men who had the last watch shivered in the damp air, and looked for the first sign of the coming sun. The village was not visible, but there was no sound from that direction. The men were miserable, fighting to stay awake. They knew that if they were attacked, they must give the alarm, and they would be the first to meet the enemy. Their dogs were stretched out in the grass, sound asleep. They strained their eyes and ears to catch the slightest sight or sound. As the eastern sky began to shed light on the earth, they heard a click. It was the sound of two spears striking. Then they saw them: a hundred spears like lightning in the half-risen sun!

They men began shouting the warning, and in a minute they were joined by sixty armed men led by the fearless Jephthah.

"Attack! Attack!" he shouted.

As his men split themselves into two groups, and raced to the sides of the oncoming army, the enemy was thrown into confusion by the movement, and hesitated for just a second too long. In three minutes twenty of the enemy lay on the ground, some dead, and some wounded. When the clanging of metal stopped, and the shouting of combat ceased, the other villagers rushed out to the battle field with great grief and consternation. They searched through the fallen for loved ones while the surviving members of the army began carrying their wounded back to the village. Chaos reigned on the field, but Jephthah regrouped his men, and led them back to their camp, carrying two that had been wounded. They were not jubilant. Their mood was one of regret. They had not come to this place for war, and they did not want to kill, but if they had to, they would. They heard sounds of mourning all day, mingled with the sound of shovels digging graves. They built a makeshift altar of stones and earth, and offered sacrifices of pigeons and turtle doves. They prayed that God would forgive their violence, and give the village peace.

"We may be forced to fight for our lives from now on," he told Tamar that evening.

"We must think of our children."

"Yes. We will defend ourselves when we must."

"How long will we remain here?" Tamar rested against a cushion, and wove a basket of small branches.

"We have earned this place with the shedding of much blood, and we will stay here until the food becomes hard to find. Now I must go see about Dodo. He has a bad wound."

As he walked to Dodo's tent, he noticed the somber mood of the camp. His men were vain men with no ambition except to be left to themselves, but they were forced into a bloody fight they did not want. There were heathen men among them, but most were Jews who disliked the idolatrous people around them. Even in the dusk there were sounds of sorrow from the field where the encounter had taken place. He told the men there was no need to post a guard for the night. There would be no more trouble from these people. There were more skirmishes with other towns and villages, however, and Jephthah became a skilled leader of warriors.

Tamar's Baby

One day Tamar discovered that she was with child. Jephthah was filled with joy. When the little girl was born the camp threw a celebration, and they named the child Anna after Tamar's mother. Jephthah was so happy he would sit for hours holding the baby on his lap admiring her. He didn't know much Scripture, but what he knew he taught the little girl, and she grew to love God and trust Him. Jephthah knew Israel's history quite well, for it intrigued him. The little girl had grown up to be a young woman of sixteen when the Ammonites declared war on Israel, and the Israelites found themselves without a suitable leader. Jephthah heard about the intentions of the Ammonites, but he had enough problems of his own. Besides, his half-brothers deserved to serve a little as slaves to the Ammonites for the way they had treated him. Jephthah hated himself for having such thoughts, but he couldn't help it. He asked God to forgive him.

The Visit

The elders of Israel had a meeting and decided that Jephthah was their only hope. *Some hope*, they thought, Jephthah would make demands on them that would not be very conducive to their happiness. He would demand to be made judge over Israel, and the thought was repugnant to them.

The oldest elder rubbed his salt and pepper beard and breathed a long sigh, "We are not well prepared for war against these Ammonites."

The circle of men sat on the ground with legs crossed, silently, hoping upon hope that someone could come up with a better idea. Several of Jephthah's half-brothers were among the elders, and they didn't relish the thought of having to go to Jephthah on bended knees.

At last one of the brothers spoke, "Surely, we can find a more suitable leader than Jephthah." He growled the name with contempt.

"I'm waiting for somebody to tell me who. Are you prepared to lead Israel to war?"

The brother shuddered at the thought. "I have my business to attend to," he retorted, glad he had an excuse.

The men continued to sit silently in thought as the fire consumed the knots fed to it. They knew that there was no alternative. Not a single man was willing, or able, to step into a general's shoes and command men to wade into a bloody battle. The thought made their stomachs threaten to turn on their lunches.

"What if Jephthah rejects our plea?" one asked.

"We'll not think of that until we ask him," replied the old man whose name was Jacob.

"Who will go to find him and ask him?"

The men looked at each other, and squirmed fearfully, hoping they could escape the task.

"We will all go. We cannot afford to have Jephthah think this is not an important matter." That word came like a slap in the mouth.

The next morning the elders met at the gate of Mizpeh, every man hating to spend days on camels, and losing money every day. They hated the thought of facing this wild ruffian who was Israel's only hope. The half-brothers were especially overcome with consternation; not even able to eat their breakfast. It was a large group with servants and pack donkeys to carry their supplies. There was no levity among the men as they snapped at each other, and complained about everything they could think of. They kicked donkeys and servants alike, venting their anger on helpless ankles and legs. Jerking halters, and shoving servants only increased their rage. Nothing went right.

They had only an idea of Jephthah's whereabouts. He never stayed in one place very long, and Tob was a mountainous area. Nevertheless, they had this task forced upon them; and they had to do it or serve the Ammonites. Jacob wearily rode a camel, drifting off to sleep in spite of being rudely shaken by the camel's plunging steps. None of the men were accustomed to riding donkeys very far, and they soon became miserable as saddles or bare backs crushed their muscles into a mass of hurt that added to their dismay.

For days they searched for Jephthah. It was like hunting a flea. Every time they were about to put a finger on him, he was somewhere else. Servants became exhausted with the constant bickering and complaining; some became sick; and others suffered injuries. Food ran short because they were on the trail of a large band who consumed almost everything the countryside could produce. Some animals became sick or crippled and had to be abandoned, much to the chagrin of the owners.

At last the men came in sight of the shabby tent camp commanded by Jephthah, and hoped they could catch him this time. Early in the morning as Jephthah's people were breaking camp the elders approached. A lookout saw them as they came and sounded an alert. Jephthah squinted into the early morning sun to determine if his band needed to prepare for combat or company. He couldn't believe his eyes as he recognized his brothers with haggard faces bowing before him. They showed the wear and tear of the trail as they handed him gifts, and begged him to parlay with them.

Jephthah showed great restraint as he welcomed all the elders to sit at his fire, and share some poor tea made from roots. He signaled his wife to go about preparing the camp's meager food for a banquet. They could ill afford a full meal, but Jephthah was determined that his brothers would not know that, even though the camp was so shabby the fact was evident to an observer. Tamar took charge, and began giving orders to the women to stop preparing to move and busy themselves about slaughtering goats and baking bread. Warm milk was given to the guests to refresh them, and they got down to business.

The visitors sat quietly for the space of thirty or forty minutes until the old man raised a jeweled hand and spoke.

"Has the God of our fathers been kind to you, Jephthah?"

"He has blessed me with a wife and daughter and many happy things," Jephthah replied with utmost courtesy as he motioned to his captains to sit in the circle.

"We will not tarry with the reason for our being here, Jephthah. You have heard that the Ammonites have declared war on us, have you not?"

"I have."

"Jephthah, you are the only hope of Israel as we have no one else who can lead our armies into battle."

Jephthah fixed his eyes on the oldest of his half brothers: the one who had ordered him out of his home long ago. The man dropped his eyes to the tiny blaze in the center of the circle. Jephthah's anger was cooled by the passage of time, but still he had to say a prayer in his heart that God would help him to behave righteously toward them.

"I have all this people to care for, and I cannot take time out to fight Israel's war."

"Jephthah, Israel's war is your war. You are a member of the tribe of Manasseh. You and your people will not be spared if Israel falls."

Jephthah sat silently for a few minutes while his thoughts gathered into a tight bunch so he could manage them. He felt a glimmer of gladness that these men had sought him out, and had appealed to him for help.

"Are you prepared to employ my men, and provide for their families, and treat us as equals?"

"We want your men to come, and we will provide their needs."

One of Jephthah's captains leaned close. and whispered in his ear.

"Are you prepared to make me a judge over Israel?"

All the elders were thrown into confusion by the question, and began to whisper among themselves. They had anticipated the possibility of the request, but they had not seriously considered it.

"Jephthah, how much power do you expect to have?"

"How much power does a judge have?"

More frantic whispering.

"We have no option." Jacob conceded.

"My men will serve as officers in Israel's army."

The elders had to agree to all of Jephthah's terms, and the more they agreed, the worse they felt.

Jephthah did not trust this delegation. His brothers had shown him no respect, and the others behaved as if they were dealing with people far below their level.

"You must be aware that I will enforce my terms with the edge of the sword. Betray me, and you will have an enemy on your hands much more dangerous that the Amorites."

The banquet came off in the middle of the afternoon, but there was little mirth among those attending, except that the servants and some of Jephthah's lesser men went off to themselves and had a good time, wrestling, racing, high jumping, and telling stories. The next morning the camp loaded up, and set out on the long trudge back to Mizpah.

Jephthah and his band were escorted back to Mizpah where he was welcomed by the citizens, and made captain over the host of their armies. He inspected the soldiers, and as he examined the bright young faces with the budding beards, he became almost despondent. He knew what warfare would do to these innocent young men. Like any great general he did not want to throw these young men into the butchery of battle where they would have to kill or be killed. All night he walked the dirt floor of his quarters, and looked into the future. Just before dawn he called for four of his lieutenants, and handed them a message he had composed. Carefully, he instructed them about their mission.

"And Jephthah sent messengers unto the king of the children of Ammon, saying, What hast thou to do with me, that thou art come against me to fight in my land?" (Judges 11:12).

All day he prayed that Mezpah might be spared from war with the Ammonites. He had no thoughts of victory and glory, only the dread of men being killed and injured. His staff gathered, and the men talked of strategy and tactics. Some of the younger officers were eager to go into battle, but most shared Jephthah's feelings at this point in time.

Jephthah's Daughter

Anna hummed a pretty little tune she made up all by herself as she busied about her little bedroom. She loved to keep all of her things in perfect order, and she was careful to dust everything (there was always plenty of dust), and make sure all of her clothes were in their proper place. Her father had become a very famous man in Gilead, and she must do her part to be worthy of him. He was the commander of Gilead's armies that were now engaged in battle with the awful Ammonites. She was so proud of him! He had been terribly abused when he was a boy: his brothers had driven him out of their home because he was only a half-brother. When he was a grown man they had to beg him to return because he had become a very skilled soldier; and they needed him to fight the Ammonites that were threatening their security.

She was familiar with the story. The tale of Lot and his narrow escape from Sodom was well known. That was when Lot's wife was turned to a pillar of stone because she looked back at Sodom. Lot and two of his daughters wound up in a cave near Zoar. The daughters made their father drunk, and used him to conceive children. The older daughter had a son whom she named Moab. The younger daughter had a son, and she named him Ben-ammi. Ben-ammi became the father of the Ammonites. When God dealt with the Ammonites He never forgot they were the descendants of Lot who, in spite of his backsliding, was a nephew of Abraham, and a man of faith. The Ammonites settled a portion of land east of the Sea of Galilee. Evidently, there were not many of these people, but they were numerous enough to present the Jews with a very real and present threat.

About three hundred years before Jephthah lived, God told Moses that when the Israelites came near the Ammonites, they were not to distress them nor meddle with them. Their land was their possession, and God intended for them to live in peace and security. The children of Ammon were a wicked, idolatrous people, knowing not God, but He knew them: and He would protect them because of Abraham and Lot. *Even the ungodly descendants of a righteous man are blessed by God,* Anna thought.

When came time for the Israelites to take Canaan, the tribes of Gad and Reuben, and half the tribe of Manasseh chose to settle on the east side of the Jordan River (or just northeast of the Dead Sea, depending on which map you look at.). Gad's possession would be north of Reuben's. During the conquest God gave the tribe of Gad permission to take half of the Ammonite's land. Now the Ammonites were determined to take back the land they had lost. The citizens of Gilead were just as determined to keep it. That is why the people and princes went to find Jephthah.

Anna's mother, too, was busy with her household duties. She had heard rumors that the Ammonites were losing skirmishes on the field of battle, and soon the war would be over; and her husband would be coming home. Tamar had to be prepared all the time for guests because of Jephthah's prominence; and often she had to console families who had lost sons and husbands in the war. She was giving orders to her bakers who were busy kneading dough, their arms powdered with flour, when suddenly there was the rattle of a horse's hooves in the courtyard; and they heard a servant's excited voice cry,

"It's a messenger from the field!"

Jephthah's daughter heard the shout, and with anxiety and joy mingling together in the cup of her emotions, dashed through the door and out into the bright sunlight as the rider brought his mount to a gravel-scattering halt in the courtyard. The lean young messenger sat astride a wiry horse, his face wet with perspiration and bright with excitement. The horse was white with a lather of sweat, and heaving with the exertion of the long run, but the happy radiance of the messenger's countenance dispelled instantly all uncertainty about his mission.

"The battle's won!" shouted the gasping young rider, and he gulped air for another shout, "the battle's won! The Ammonite heathen are defeated, and the army of the God of Israel is marching home. Captain Jephthah will be here before the evening!

Jephthah's daughter and her mother embraced each other, and danced around in a circle while the servants clapped their hands with joy.

"Father's coming home! Father's coming home!" Anna shouted exuberantly over and over as she clapped her hands together and leaped around joyfully.

"Yes, we must prepare a feast for him," her mother replied, her face shining with the glow of joy. "But first, let us stop and thank the LORD God of our fathers for this great deliverance, for He has again delivered us out the hands of our enemies."

The group knelt, and gave thanks to God for what He had done for them.

"I must run and tell my friends," Jephthah's daughter called to her mother over her shoulder as she raced down the garden path, her black hair flying on the wind; then; suddenly remembering that she was running from her duties, she stopped, and faced her mother. "Oh, Mother, may I? I won't take long."

Her mother waved her on, then gave orders for the messenger to be cared for, and hastened toward her kitchen, giving enthusiastic orders to the servants swirling around her. Animals must be slaughtered, chickens killed, fish were taken out of storage, oranges and apples peeled. The kitchen was a hot, bustling ant hill.

People began gathering as Jephthah's daughter and her friends laughed and cried together while she told them about the return of the army. They had not heard the good news, and the story coming from the daughter of the captain placed an authority on it that lent it greater satisfaction. Most of the onlookers, and the girls had fathers and brothers in the army. Anna had no brothers or sisters of her own, and so her friends were especially important to her. They were like her, too, for they had the same religious beliefs; and their parents were all close friends.

A large crowd of children quickly gathered with everyone trying to talk at the same time, and then adults, too, joined the crowd. Soon the whole city was filled with the electricity of excitement. Happy expectations gladdened every heart now, but some would be made very sad by news from the army of a soldier's death as the dead were identified and messages sent.

"I must go," cried Anna after a while, "Mother needs my help, and I must make myself ready for my father's arrival."

She hastened back toward her home with heart racing with excitement. She loved her father very much; for since he had had such a bad childhood, he had worked hard to be a good parent. He was kind to her, and always seemed to make her feel very important. What could she do to make his homecoming especially happy?

"Oh, the tophs," she remembered. "My timbrels that he gave me! I will watch for him, and when he comes through our gate I will go running out, singing and playing my tophs, and I will dance for joy."

Her mind was dizzy with delight as she entered the house and hurried to the kitchen. The place was an overheated beehive with coals blazing and pots boiling as Mother directed the servants in the preparation of the feast: a calf was being roasted, bread and cakes were in the ovens, and the air was rich with the delicious aroma of cooking food.

"Go gather flowers for the table, dear," her mother said, and at once Anna took her basket, and started for the garden.

"Only the sweetest blossoms will have the honor of serving our table this day," she sang as she began cutting the stems. "My father is coming home victorious over the enemies of the LORD our God."

The flowers seemed more lovely than she had ever seen them. The roses were bright, and the narcissus, and the colchicum, and the perky crocus, and the lilac. The oleander turned her basket into a hilarious burst of color. She even clipped a few yellowish blossoms from the rue which sent its sharp odor up her nose, and made her mouth water.

"Cool off, little flower," she laughed, and then wondered if it would not be a little too loud for the occasion, but decided that a few buds would add an appetizing bit of zest. With her basket loaded, she returned to the house where she collected the alabaster vases and brass bowls, and arranged them on the long table. Then with the most meticulous care, she sorted the flowers into bouquets in the vessels on the table, reveling in the rich perfumes. Even a great general would love such beautiful flowers.

She took her time arranging them until she was satisfied, and then stood back to view her work. The colors were almost dazzling in their rich beauty, and she was very pleased with her arrangements. At last, she was content, and with a little twinge of anxiety, wondered what time it was. The messenger had said that her father would arrive before the evening; and she was sure it must be near four o'clock.

Quickly, she turned toward the door, and flew to her bed room where she happily took her clothes from her cedar chest, and laid them on her bed. Swift strokes with a brush smoothed her hair. She washed and anointed her body with perfumed olive oil; cinnamon in her hair; cassia on her arms and shoulders, and then a tinny-smelling sack of aloes was tied to the linen girdle around her waist. She splashed her choicest perfumes about her person, and finally secured a flower in her hair; and her favorite necklace around her neck. She checked her silken mantle which was over her left shoulder, and under her right arm, and for a moment gazed at her image in her mirror of brass. She wished that she were pretty, but she had to accept the homey face in the mirror as her own face. Her inspection was cut short by the rattling sound of a chariot and a diver's rough voice.

Anna's heart leaped into her throat as she snatched her tophs, shook them over her head, and recklessly dashed toward the front door. One of the maidens was about to run through the door, but Anna playfully pushed her aside and ran out into the courtyard, playing her tophs and dancing in a frenzy of joy.

"My father is home! My darling father is home from the battle with the hated enemies of the LORD our God. My father is home victorious over the heathen. They are defeated! They have fallen! They are no more!"

Mrs. Jephthah ran through the door and into her husband's arms rejoicing. Anna rushed to join them, but instantly realized that her father was not rejoicing. His face was twisted into a mass of anguish. He pushed her mother back, and tore his clothes as he burst into loud wailing. Anna was stunned: smitten silent by the appearance of her father and his tears. Had she done some terrible thing? Was she improperly attired? But no improper attire could bring on such consternation as she saw in her father's face. What was wrong? Her joy plunged from its height; and her soul was filled with alarm.

Her father trembled like a winter leaf on a barren branch, and a paroxysm of torment shook his huge body from head to foot. The great sword hanging from his wide girdle rattled in its scabbard as the mighty general blubbered like a lost child; then gouged into the hard earth when he fell upon his knees and wailed like a distressed woman. The warrior tore his clothes and cried out to God for mercy. The officers of his staff stood around aghast at the sudden outburst from their leader, and knew that some calamity had suddenly befallen him that was more than they could know or understand. They didn't dare speak or interfere.

Tamar fell to her knees beside her husband, and buried her face in her hands; her horrified soul pierced with fear and perplexity, while Jephthah released all the sorrows of his heart. Sorrows that had built up during the bloody war, and indeed, during a hard and bitter life. This man had not cried since he was a small, rejected lad; but now he was so reduced that he cried about all the things in his heart which had deserved tears, but had been denied them. He cried for his prostitute mother, whom he knew not. He cried because he had been driven from his home, and grew up in far away Tob as a homesick orphan. He wept for every one of his soldiers who had been slain or wounded in battle. He saw the beardless faces, stained with dirt and blood, grimacing in pain as swords, and spears, and axes, and horses' teeth and hooves tore their flesh and shattered their bones. The dead stared into eternity with lifeless eyes while the living struggled to live. He wept loud to drown out the awful sounds of screams of dying men and horses; the clash of iron, and the deadly hiss of arrows: sounds and scenes that were locked into his memory banks to haunt him forever. The brine stained his cheeks; soaked the massive beard; and made little pools on the sandy soil of his garden path. He wept until the spring of tears ran dry, then, fell exhausted in the dirt. Anna joined her father's wailing, though she knew not why he wept. Her tophs lay silent among the pebbles of the courtyard. Her oiled face was streaked with tears: tears that flowed she knew not why but that her father wept.

The officers around the great General Jephthah slipped away to the outside of the wall where they stood in embarrassed silence, knowing not what was the cause of the sudden change from joy to woe, or what to do about it. As men they could fight men, but emotions left them confused and humiliated. They had no doubts about the manhood of their leader, and they sympathized with him for whatever had brought him to this state of grief.

At long last, the man raised himself to his knees where he looked at the trembling figure of his distraught daughter standing before him.

34 *"And Jephthah came to Mizpeh unto his house, and, behold, his daughter came out to meet him with timbrels and with dances: and she was his only child; beside her he had neither son nor daughter.*

35 *"And it came to pass, when he saw her, that he rent his clothes, and said, Alas, my daughter! thou hast brought me very low, and thou art one of them that trouble me: for I have opened my mouth UNTO THE LORD, and I cannot go back."* (Judges 11:34-35).

"Before we went into battle, I vowed unto the LORD. I did not intend to offer you, my dear, but in my zeal and stress I did not realize that you would surely be the first thing out of my house to greet me when I returned. In that I am at fault. But perhaps God wanted my best, and who could blame Him for that? God gave me the victory, and now Daughter, you are a devoted thing."

Jephthah's wife reeled back in disbelief, and leaned on her servants. The daughter was horrified as her father's words sank into her mind, but strangely relieved that she had not done something to cause his grief. She stepped close to her father as the man pushed himself slowly to his feet, looking at her with interminable woe. She took his hands, and looked sweetly into his tear-streaked face, and said,

"My father, if thou hast opened thy mouth unto the LORD, do to me according to that which proceeded out of thy mouth: forasmuch as the LORD hath taken vengeance for thee of thine enemies, even of the children of Ammon."

The mighty warrior, with hands hardened and trained to grasp shield and sword, held the tender hands of his child, and melted into a softness more delicate than moonlight. His brawny body shook so that his armor clattered. He looked through his tears, and those in the eyes of his daughter, and whispered,

"We will not dishonor the God of our fathers by cowardice or rebellion." The raven head of the daughter nodded her assent.

"But my husband," cried the wife looking up with piteous eyes, "why did you vow whatever came out the house first as a burnt offering? We do not keep sheep in our house!" She stooped and took a handful of dust, and threw it into the air above her head.

"I cannot explain, Wife," replied the man, "I was surely carried away in a moment of enthusiasm. I feared for my young men. The LORD my God will forgive me my lack of wisdom, and He will deliver us from this bitter experience."

The officers had quietly slipped back through the gate into the courtyard when they heard their chief's crying subside, and watched the scene in silent expectation.

"Yes, but God had a purpose for that, and never intended that Abraham would kill his son. And Abraham knew that, too." Of course, Jephthah knew that before she said it, but he did not yield to her pleas.

"In our law, Jephthah," dared one of the generals to speak, "we are told that *when a man shall make a singular vow, the person shall be for the LORD by estimation.*" You can redeem your daughter for ten shekels." (Leviticus 27:5)

"I am aware of that, and that is what I intended to do, but I added that it would be a burnt offering. She is devoted to the LORD and is most holy. She cannot be redeemed," Jephthah groaned (Leviticus 27:28,29).

"Perhaps, sir," the general continued fearfully, "you should talk to the priest."

"Most surely, I will do that," replied Jephthah.

"But you cannot kill our daughter, Jephthah," wailed Mrs. Jephthah. "She is all we have, and it would be murder, Jephthah. Your sin of murder will be greater than breaking a foolish vow. That law does not mean you have to offer a human sacrifice as a burnt offering."

"Away, Woman!" commanded the husband, harshly, "the vow is made and cannot be broken."

The horror of the situation was too great for the wife, and she slipped to the earth in blessed unconsciousness. Her servants caught her and carried her into the house. Anna pulled her thoughts together, and wiped her stained, blazing face with her hands, and pleaded with her father: "

"Let this thing be done for me: let me alone two months, that I may go up and down upon the mountains, and bewail my virginity, I and my fellows, ..."

Jephthah looked long into the sweet, submissive face of his darling child - his only child - and his heart nearly burst with love for her. "Truly, my child, you do well to honor God's Law which commands children to *'honor thy father and mother'*, and though I did not well to dishonor it by making a vow without much prayer and supplication unto the LORD, go, and do as you have said. Only wait until I have talked to the priest tomorrow."

The other servants disappeared quietly into the house as Jephthah and his daughter started slowly toward it. The flowers in their vases on the table were wilted; their perfumes dissipated, and the food cold and gray and untouched. In her room, Anna silently untied the perfume sack from her belt, and despondently dropped it on the table. She took off her fine clothes, numbly folding them on her bed. The timbrels had been picked up by one of the maidens, and returned to their chests mute, their happy chattering forgotten. With fainting heart, she bound a change of raiment in a small bundle, and placed it in a corner to wait the time when her father would release her to make her journey of sorrows. She'd make more preparations tomorrow.

The songs of the night birds wafted through her window as usual, but the sounds were strangely distant and discordant. In a few hours her cotton sheet that covered her tiny bed was sweaty and wrinkled, wrapped around her like a shroud. She could not sleep, but turned like a door on its hinges back and forth. Often she would rise and tiptoe to the pitcher on the little table in the corner to drink of its tepid contents. In spite of her excellent health, she was sick; her feelings changing from queasiness in her stomach to dry mouth to agonizing headache to lightning-like flashes around her heart. She thought she might die, and for her father's sake: hoped she would.

Terror froze the blood supply to her heart. There were phantoms in the room, and ghost-like shadows concealed unknown dangers in the corners. She felt the cold breath of death. She remembered seeing the skull of an animal one time in a field outside of town, and she wondered what her skull would look like. Would it be as plain as her face? Then she remembered that her body would be burned, and there would be no skeleton. As the midnight hour passed, she looked up from her soggy pillow through her open window to the stars sparkling above. How could they twinkle when the whole world was dripping tears? It was weirdly odd, as if nothing had changed. Would the stars glitter like that after she was dead? Would her little bed chamber be the same after she was gone? Would her spirit come here to haunt it? She knew better than that. The room would be locked up, and never entered again. The long ebony locks of her hair wrapped around her neck and face, seeming to become her enemies bent on strangling her.

She remembered the ancient story of Cain's offering, and how God was displeased with it (Genesis 4). Would God be angry with her daddy for offering her, as God was angry with Cain for offering fruits? No, she decided, Cain must have known he was offering the wrong thing. He just expected God to be happy with what he was willing to offer rather than offer what God had commanded. Her father was obeying the Law of God. She remembered Abraham offering Isaac, and a small glimmer of optimism beamed in her heart only to quickly chill and die. Almost at a standstill did the night move. Occasionally, a wakened cock would crow, giving the false hope that dawn was about to appear. She remembered a hundred things that she had not thought of since they happened: a cut toe, her fourth birthday, her mother teaching her how to brush her hair, her first puppy. Dozens of Bible stories passed through her mind, reminding her that in all of life's difficulties that God had control. Noah passed through death to a new life; and a new world that was much worse than the one he left; but though the world had changed, God had not. He is Alpha and Omega: the Beginning and the End.

After an interminable night of horrors, the dawn finally pinkened the eastern sky, and the roosters began crowing in earnest. Jephthah's daughter breathed a prayer of thanks and worship, and lay quietly, waiting for sounds that meant that the household had come to life. She was exhausted: much more weary than when she went to bed. She had slept for brief intervals during the morning, but she had not been aware of it. Soon, though, she became so uncomfortable that she got up, and went to her basin, and washed her face. Slowly, she dressed herself, and sat down and softly sang a lovely psalm.

"THE LORD is my shepherd; I shall not want. [2]He maketh me to lie down in green pastures: he leadeth me beside the still waters. [3]He restoreth my soul: he leadeth me in the paths of righteousness for his name' sake. [4]Yea, though I walk through the valley of the shadow of death, I will fear no evil: for thou art with me; thy rod and thy staff they comfort me. [5]Thou preparest a table before me in the presence of mine enemies: thou anointest my head with oil; my cup runneth over. [6]Surely goodness and mercy shall follow me all the days of my life: and I will dwell in the house OF THE LORD for ever."

When she heard noises of others stirring about in the house, she went into the kitchen where her mother was stoking the smoldering ashes of the night before. Mrs. Jephthah looked around and rose to embrace her daughter, and both wept softly for a minute or two before stepping back. "I'm sure there was not a soul in this house who slept last night," said the older woman. Her baggy, red eyes were testimony to her miserable night. "Your father walked the floor all night. He finally laid down completely exhausted just before daylight. Did you sleep at all?"

"Not very much, Mother. Will Father see the priest this morning?"

"Yes."

Servants began coming into the kitchen, and then Jephthah arrived. He embraced his wife, and murmured affectionate sounds in her ears. Then he hugged his daughter.

Food was prepared, but little was eaten, and few words were spoken. The servants said nothing. Jephthah was dressed in his best civilian clothes for his interview with the priest. He ate a piece of bread sipped in honey and butter, and drank some warm milk. He rose from the table, and walked out without a word; his personal servant on his heels, carrying a small lamb for a sacrifice.

Jephthah and the Priest

As Jephthah walked through the unpaved streets toward the priest's house, he met few people, but those he met greeted him with a sort of reverent fear. He acknowledged each one with great courtesy, and little indication of the anguish that was burning in his soul. The citizens of Mizpeh knew that without his leadership, they would all be servants of the hated Ammonites that morning.

Jephthah knocked on the door of the priest's house, and waited until the door opened. The wife of the priest stood in the open door with a tiny toddler wearing nothing but a cotton diaper clinging to her skirt, and peeping around at him with great round, dark eyes. The woman threw her hand over her mouth when she recognized the great captain of Israel's armies. Then without a word she fled through the house to fetch her husband, dragging the tot who could barely stay on his feet. In spite of his misery, Jephthah enjoyed just a glimmer of mirth; and a slight grin raised the corners of his mouth. He waited patiently at the open door, standing straight and tall like a cedar of Lebanon, his military discipline refusing to allow his shoulders to droop under their load of concern. When the priest at last arrived at the door, Jephthah understood why his arrival had been so long coming. The man was probably preparing for the day when Jephthah knocked, and the announcement of the captain's arrival had thrown him into a quandary. His cheeks above his beard were ablaze with awe and embarrassment. The shoulders of his threadbare robe were back too far, indicating that he had thrown it on quickly and had not pulled the shoulders and sleeves into place. He was a young man of fine, handsome countenance, but almost as rattled as his wife in the presence of the captain of the LORD's army. But he quickly collected his scattered wits, and motioned for Jephthah to enter his house as he stepped back and said,

"Come in, Captain Jephthah, our home is yours, and we are honored by your visit."

Jephthah lowered his bare head to clear the door, and stepped in. The wife had been frantically arranging the chairs, and just barely escaped the room with the baby still hanging on for dear life as the men entered the room. The priest motioned to a chair, and after his guest was seated, he sat down.

"Our people all over Gilead owe you a great debt of gratitude, Captain Jephthah," the priest said. "If Israel were destroyed, there would be no Messiah."

"The victory is the LORD's, Rabbi," answered Jephthah without false modesty. It was simply the truth.

The priest had heard about Jephthah's vow as had everybody in Mizpeh, but he dared not breach the subject. He was quite sure that the reason for Jephthah's visit was to seek help in carrying out his vow. Jephthah sat silently, dreading to talk about the matter, especially with a man so young. He had to fight a battle with his emotions, and struggle to hold back the flood of tears that threatened to wash his face as he was forced to come face to face with the matter. The long silence filled the priest with trepidation, and he had to work hard to resist the urge to squirm. He felt the anguish in his guest's heart, and this added to his emotional discomfort, and almost reduced him to tears. At last, Jephthah took great deep breaths, and grunted as he cleared his throat.

"Rabbi, as you must know, I made a vow to God before our great campaign against the Ammonites, and now I am very low, for my vow requires me to offer my only child to the LORD as a burnt offering," Jephthah said slowly, struggling with every word, and having to force them from his throat.

The priest allowed a long minute to pass as Jephthah recovered from his confession. He looked at the bearded face of a man who had given orders to men that placed their lives in jeopardy - the face of a man who remained unemotional when he gave orders to generals. But now the face was tear-stained and crimson with a personal conflict that could well kill him before it was over.

"I will have my wife bring some water, Jephthah, would you like some bread and milk?"

"I would like some water, please, nothing else."

"Wife," the priest called through the house, but before he could say anything else, his wife came through the door with a pitcher of water and cups. She had lost the infant somewhere along the way. He was somewhere in the house gurgling over some new-found trinket. She did her duty quickly; and hastily left the room. The priest poured water into a cup, and handed it to Jephthah who drank it all, and nodded his thanks.

"Tell me, Jephthah, what you will."

"You know I was abused and cast out of my home by my half-brothers when I was only a very young man," Jephthah began. "I fled to Tob up north, and there I became involved with vain men. We went about hunting and gathering to live, but my soul was vexed, and I prayed that God would deliver me from such a dilemma."

Jephthah took another long drink of water, and being more at ease, having gotten into his story, he continued with less strain on himself.

"The elders of Gilead came to me one day, and told me that the Ammonites had again attacked our people, and they wanted me to take charge of the campaign against them. For eighteen years the Ammonites had harassed Israel, and it was time to settle the matter."

*"And it came to pass in process of time, that the children of Ammon made war against **Israel**. And it was so, that when the children of Ammon made war against **Israel**, the elders of Gilead went to fetch Jephthah out of the land of Tob:"* (Judges 11:4,5).

"I confess that the bitterness in my heart caused me to respond in a selfish way, for I required the elders to promise me that if I led the armies, and was victorious, that I would be made the head of Gilead. I was sure that I could bring some security and stability to our land."

The priest's little toddler crawled through the door, and Jephthah was pleased when the baby came to his feet, and looked up into his face. The child brightened into a pixy smile, and to his father's horror, pulled himself to his feet by holding to the general's tunic. As the priest lunged forward to take up the child, Jephthah leaned down and took him up in his arms. The child giggled and wriggled in Jephthah's lap as Jephthah hugged him, and kissed his chubby cheeks, and wished in a secret chamber of his heart that Anna had been a boy. This baby boy would someday be a priest as his daddy was.

"Jephthah, I - "

"No, Rabbi," said Jephthah, "he is a comfort to me. What a beautiful child."

Then the mother stuck her head around the doorjamb looking for her wandering baby. She gasped when she saw him on Jephthah's lap, and ran into the room, grabbed the tot, and ran out. Jephthah was sorry to see him go, but he knew that the parents were afraid he would wet on their distinguished guest; a privilege reserved for infants.

There was silence for the space a minute or two while the memory of the incident faded.

"I returned to Mizpeh in Gilead, and sent emissaries to the king of the Ammonites pleading with him to desist in his wars against us, but he would not hear."

"Then the Spirit of the LORD came upon Jephthah, and he passed over Gilead, and Manasseh, and passed over Mizpeh of Gilead, and from Mizpeh of Gilead he passed over [unto]the children of Ammon Ammon." Judges 11:29.

"As the time of battle grew near, though, the Spirit of the LORD had moved upon me, I was much concerned for the men and boys who were about to die, both my own and those of the children of Ammon. In my fear and stress, Rabbi, I,

'vowed a vow unto the LORD, and said, If thou shalt without fail deliver the children of Ammon into mine hands, Then it shall be, that whatsoever cometh forth of the doors of my house to meet me, when I return in peace from the children of Ammon, shall surely be the LORD's, and I will offer it up for a burnt offering'."

Jephthah sat with his head down for a long moment as the priest absorbed what he had heard. The priest wished that he had been born into a tribe other than the tribe of Levi, for as a descendant of that great patriarch, he was destined to fill the office of a priest. But he had no options. His wishing would change nothing. He was confronted with this duty, and he must fill it. He must do it right.

"Captain Jephthah, did you intend this offering to be a devoted thing, or was it a singular vow?" the priest asked.

In spite of the consequences of his answer, there was something within Jephthah that forced him to tell the truth. He was not speaking only to a man in a priest's garb: he was talking also to the LORD God.

"I intended my vow to be a devoted thing." Jephthah knew that when he said that, that this man would, in a few weeks, end his daughter's life on Earth.

The son of Levi rose from his chair, and beckoning Jephthah to follow, walked to a large table where there lay a beautifully ornamented scroll, which, in spite of its age and wear, was a work of art to be admired. Reverently, the priest covered his head, and unfastened the cord that bound the roll. He unrolled the long document until he came to the Book of Leviticus. There were no chapters or verses, but the Jewish rabbi knew exactly where the words were located. His finger not quite touching the vellum, the priest pointed to the solemn words:

"Notwithstanding no devoted thing, that a man shall devote UNTO THE LORD of all that he hath, both of man and beast, and of the field of his possession, shall be sold or redeemed: every devoted thing is most holy UNTO THE LORD. ²⁹None devoted, which shall be devoted of men, shall be redeemed; but shall surely be put to death." (Leviticus 27:28,29).

"This, Jephthah, as you know, is the Law of the LORD. It cannot be broken. Had you made a singular vow, you could have redeemed your daughter. Under the terms of the Law regarding devoted things, you must offer her."

"But did God not forbid the offering of children as burnt offerings?" Jephthah grabbed the last straw.

The rabbi rolled part of the scroll back until h came to the passage. There he read the words of the LORD.

"Again thou shalt say to the children of Israel, Whosoever he be of the children of Israel, or of the strangers that sojourn in Israel, that giveth

any of his seed unto Molech; he shall surely be put to death: the people of the land shall stone him with stones." (Leviticus 20:2).

"You are not offering your offering to a god of the Canaanites, Captain Jephthah, but to Jehovah. Offering any sacrifice to an idol is an abomination, but the Canaanites brought such great numbers of babies into the world by their immoral worship that they had to dispose of them some way, and so they burned them."

"I saw such a ritual one time," Jephthah added. "A family of Canaanites had built a new house, and they sealed a jug containing the ashes of a sacrificed infant in the foundation of the house for good luck and to appease their god Molech."

"A horrible business, sacrificing children to idols," added the priest before he continued.

The last glimmer of hope was now gone for Jephthah. His daughter belonged to the LORD, and the way to give her was through an altar fire as a burnt offering.

"Rabbi, has there ever been such a thing done in Israel?"

"It has never been done. There may have been persons who made such a vow involving humans, but none has ever gone through with the sacrifice. It is common for people to offer animals as devoted things."

"Do you know how to go about this?" Jephthah wanted to know.

"Yes. It will be done as any other burnt offering, and I have done thousands of them."

"I greatly fear for the health of my wife. This is even more painful for her than it is for me," Jephthah said quietly, thinking of the anguish of his companion's face.

The priest sat quietly trying to frame a response that would be appropriate. He wished with all his heart that he had studied the Law more carefully than he had. He wished that he were an older man with more experience. Though all men should be equal in his sight, he could not help being intimidated by the status of this great soldier. He determined in his heart that he would rise to this occasion, and by God's grace: handle it right. He wondered in his heart if he would be able to keep such a vow.

The priest and Jephthah did not have the indwelling Holy Spirit to comfort and guide them, because the Age of Grace was still centuries in the future. Though they lived in Gilead, they did not have the "Balm in Gilead" that the old Negro spiritual so beautifully glorifies. They did not have the light of the New Testament with its promises and hope. We cannot understand the mind set of people in those ancient days who lived without the spiritual blessings we enjoy. We study the Psalms and discover much about them, and rejoice in the great faith of some of them revealed to us in the prophets: yet we cannot place ourselves in their hearts. Jephthah's faith is magnified when we think of these things. He was not comforted by the Holy Spirit, but he did what he vowed to do in spite of the pain.

"My daughter has asked for two months to go up and down on the mountains, and mourn her virginity. When she returns, we will fulfill the vow at once."

The priest trembled at the thought, but replied, "I will offer your sacrifice for you."

The great general nodded his head, and sat silently for a breath or two on the edge of the chair, and then replied, "I will build the altar. I don't want her offered on the town altar. And I want her altar to be a memorial to her." He looked at the priest. "It must be of uncut stones?"

"An altar of earth thou shalt make unto me, and shalt sacrifice thereon thy burnt-offerings, and thy peace-offerings, thy sheep, and thine oxen: in all places where I record my name I will come unto thee, and I will bless thee. And if thou wilt make me an altar of stone, thou shalt not build it of hewn stone: for if thou lift up thy tool upon it, thou hast polluted it. Neither shall ye go up by steps unto mine altar, that thy nakedness be not discovered thereon." Exodus 20:24.

Jephthah rose up, and moved a step toward the door. He wished the tot were in the room. The priest did likewise. "We will go to the altar with your peace offering now, Captain Jephthah, if you are ready," he said.

"I am ready," Jephthah replied as they started for the door.

Jephthah's servant was patiently waiting for him outside under a tree, closely watching the little lamb as it nibbled blades of grass here and there. He picked up the little animal, and followed Jephthah and the priest to a large pile of stones in the street that looked like many animals had been burned upon it, with fire-blackened stones and ashes rendering a picture of sin and death.

Jephthah took the lamb in his arms, and said, "God, be merciful to me, a sinner."

The priest quickly severed the little head, and caught some of its blood in a basin. He sprinkled the blood on the stones of the altar, and opened the lamb's body and removed certain parts. There was much fat inside the carcass, showing that it had been well cared for. Then the priest laid the little wooly body on the wood on top of the pile of stones. He lit the fire, and they stood watching as the body was consumed by the flames. Jephthah's tunic and the priest's robe were spotted with blood, but *"without the shedding of blood shall no flesh be justified."* Jephthah had made peace with God. The little lamb has paid the cost with its life. A curse, indeed, was the Law.

Anna Departs

Anna spent a melancholy morning making preparations for her sojourn on the mountains. Her father had come home with the final word of the priest, and released her to go. She ate a light lunch, and went out to seek her three best friends. She found them sitting under a tree, talking excitedly about the events of the past two days. When Anna walked up to join them the girls got up to greet her, and the brightness of their faces was quickly changed to gray by the appearance of Anna's face.

"Anna!" exclaimed Asenath who was wont to rush in where angels fear to trod. "What's wrong?"

The girls sat mutely looking at one another with alarm in their faces while Anna gathered her emotions into tight bundles so she could control them. She sat down with her friends and sighed heavily.

"My father vowed a vow to the LORD that if God would deliver his enemies into his hands, that he would offer as a burnt whatever first came out of his house when he returned home in peace. I was the first one out to greet him," Anna told them with voice trembling with trepidation.

As she sat there looking at the ground, there was a stillness like the stillness of a tomb. Even the birds in the tree fell silent. The girls were filled with perplexity: what did Anna mean by that? It sounded so ominous. Afraid to ask, the trio sat motionless with not a sound. Even Asenath, the precocious one, was quiet.

Slowly, Anna explained to them, and Deborah asked, "What is your father going to do?"

"My father is going to offer me as a burnt offering," Anna answered. Every time she said it, the situation became more real to Anna, and she was more able to grasp it.

"But, Anna, surely your own father will not kill you," objected Miriam tearfully. She was quick to laugh: quick to cry.

"Your father is a great man, Anna, we cannot believe he would make a vow without prayer and thought," added Deborah, the intellectual, her voice conveying confidence that Jephthah was a good man who would never commit such an act.

The girls were having difficulty grasping the full meaning of what Anna was saying, and what it all meant.

"Why would your father do such a thing?" asked Asenath with horror in her voice.

"How can we understand the stress of war upon a man – and the responsibility for the lives of thousands of men – even the whole nation? How can we understand the desire of a leader to gain victory, and save as many lives as possible? We cannot understand. I know my father is a great man: he is a godly man. I also know that my father loves me. He made a clear vow to the LORD. The Scriptures say that we must not make a vow and break it, for God hath no pleasure in fools," Anna answered, hoping to convince herself as well as her friends.

"I don't understand it. It's too awful to even think about," cried Miriam, dabbing her nose with the hem of her mantle.

"A great leader should be able to handle those stresses, Anna," said Deborah. "I don't mean to be judgmental, but it seems very foolish to me."

"Why should you have to suffer for your father's mistake, Anna? That isn't fair," Miriam said, tearfully, fearfully.

"I am my father's child, Miriam, surely you could not expect me to do anything but obey him," Anna retorted.

"Abraham would have killed Isaac if God had not stopped him," added Deborah, bringing past and present together in a struggle to bring understanding to the situation.

"Do you think God will save you like He did Isaac, Anna?" Asenath wanted to know.

"I have no doubt that God could if He so chose. I am certain that my father believes that God will intervene and solve the dilemma. My father is only a man. But in any event, I will be submissive to my Father."

"Your father must believe that God will spare you as he did Isaac," Asenath added.

"I don't think he believes that I will be spared, but he would not be greatly surprised if the LORD did that. But remember that God commanded Abraham to offer Isaac," Anna replied.

"I wonder why God did that," Deborah said.

"I do not know," Anna admitted, "but I am sure it had something to do with the promised Messiah."

"It is all so hard to comprehend," murmured Miriam, still sniffing into her hem, and thinking of something beyond the immediate time and space.

"Will you go with me to mourn my virginity?" Anna asked. The girls looked at each other with dread in their faces. They were afraid to answer. At last Asenath dared to say, "We must get permission. It will be dangerous on the mountains."

"I know. You don't have to go, of course, but I need you very much," Anna replied.

Deborah put her hand on Anna's arm, and said, "I will go if my parents will permit it."

The other two girls looked at each other, and then all three got up and hurried away to their homes, leaving Anna sitting under the tree, waiting. She dreamed of the days when she was very small, and how her daddy would toss her into the air, and then hold her secure in his hard, hairy arms. *Oh, to do that again.* She was startled when Deborah spoke to her from behind. Deborah gave Anna a hand up.

"My parents told me I can go."

"I must go home and make preparations, and I will come to your house at dusk," Anna replied.

"Everyone will stay with me tonight," she said with her voice full of sympathy, "and before dawn, we will depart."

Anna's mother stayed close to her as she put together the things she would take with her, suggesting this and that for her to take along, and giving advice about how to survive on the mountains, as if she had made such a journey herself. Jephthah's wife understood the futility of resisting her husband's determination to honor his vow, but she also determined that she would resist him to the end. She had said to him what Job's wife said to Job,

"Then said his wife unto him, Dost thou still retain thine integrity? curse God, and die.
"But he said unto her, Thou speakest as one of the foolish women speaketh. What? shall we receive good at the hand of God, and shall we not receive evil? In all this did not Job sin with his lips:" (Job 2:9).

Anna would travel light. Two changes of clothes, a blanket, a bottle of olive oil, extra sandals, and some food and water, and some odds and ends were sufficient. She would take some money to buy food in villages along the way. As the dusk was settling, she said good bye to her mother, and walked away, leaving the woman shaking violently with sobs of grief and fear. One of her maidservants was with her, and she was crying also. Anna had said goodbye to her father when he left for military duty just after his return from the priest's house.

There was little conversation in Deborah's home, because Jephthah was too important in the town to be discussed - no one wanted to seem critical of him; and the whole situation was just too unreal for conversation. There was also the dread of the two long months the girls would be absent. The mountain crawled with animals of all sorts, most of them dangerous. There were shepherds who were men of uncertain reputation and behavior. There were serpents and insects which were not friendly to humans. The land was mostly desolate and dry with a scattering of villages and tribes who were strangers. The mountain was no place for four young girls alone.

Long before dawn the four girls slipped out of the house and headed toward the nearby mountain. The city was still asleep so the girls went silently, awakening not even a dog. The departure was a sad one, and no one felt like saying anything; there would be plenty of time to talk. They did not know fully what they would do or where they would go, or why, it was just a matter of being in a solitary place where they could mourn and talk, and help prepare Anna for her death.

Four Girls and a Mountain

The mountain was steep and rocky, and the cold morning air caused an occasional shiver even with their skin damp with perspiration. Here and there they could see in the dawn's brightening light shepherds watching small flocks of sheep; still huddled around the dim coals of their camp fires. By afternoon they could look down on the distant city shimmering in the rising heat. Anna wondered what her parents were doing.

The girls sat down by a large rock, and ate some bread and fruit from their bundles. A small brook provided water for drinking and bathing hot faces and hands. Anna talked while the other girls sat silently, patiently allowing her to comfort herself with her own words. As they started off again, Anna broke into tears, and all four girls sank down on stones and wept together.

And so it went for many days. They became ragged and homesick, the thought of their mothers' kitchens bringing sweet memories of good food and fellowship. They replenished their food supply at tiny villages along the way, and at the camps of poor shepherds. There were long hours when they had neither food nor drink, and their hunger brought their emotions closer the surface and they cried quicker and longer.

In the villages, curious people would gather around them to ogle them, and quiz them about why they were there. The girls would relate the story to the circle of curious people, and watch their response. Women were concerned that such a thing could be done, but the men honored Jephthah for his courage and faith. All admired Anna for her obedience, and because she was most holy to the LORD, they were reverent in her presence. Often, girls Anna's age would put their arms around her, and wail with her. To die without having a husband and children was the worst calamity that could befall a woman.

They neared one village while a small crowd of people was gathered just outside. When they got close to the group, they saw the town priest in the middle with a lamb in his arms. They stopped to watch as a man who was kneeling stood up, and took the lamb from the priest's arms. The man was weeping, and wept even louder as he placed his hand on the head of the lamb and cried out something the girls could not understand because he was so emotional. Then, with a quick motion, the priest sliced off the head of the tiny animal, and laid its carcass on the pile of wood on top of a heap of stones and dirt. Then the priest put fire to the wood, and stepped back to watch with the crowd as the lamb was consumed in the fire.

Some of the people knelt in prayer, and everybody, including our girls, shed many tears while the fire burned, and the little body slowly disappeared. The man who had put his hand on the head of the lamb, again knelt with his head down, and prayed. This lasted for more than an hour until the fire had taken away all the fuel on the pile of stones, and gradually died out, and there was only glowing red ashes. The repentant man who had offered the sacrifice slowly got to his feet, and was met by several people who embraced him, and then the group began to disperse.

Then the people noticed the strange girls, and gathered tightly around them, their necks stretching with curiosity. The priest took it upon himself to make the inquiries about whom they were, and Deborah told him the story. Not a soul left the place while the story was being told, and when it was done, everyone in the crowd had to touch Anna. The women and girls embraced her with reverence and love, not only because she was a devoted thing; but because she was the daughter of the great Jephthah who was known even in this remote mountain village. Reverently the priest's wife took Anna's hand, and said,

"My dear, you must spend this night with us, and your friends will spend the night with our neighbors."

Anna looked at her friends, and each face said, "Yes" and so she followed as the priest led the way. The other three girls were led away to different houses in the village. The priest opened his door for Anna, and she went in, followed by the priest's wife and daughter. The man went into an adjoining room to change out of his blood-spattered garments while the wife stirred her fire, and began preparing the evening meal. Soon the delicious smell of baking bread wafted out of the oven, and Anna was made glad by the memory of fresh bread.

The daughter came away from the kitchen with the explanation that her mother had sent her to entertain Anna. She sat down on the floor in front of Anna, and gazed into her face. "Oh, Anna," she said at last, "you are so brave."

"You haven't told me your name," Anna replied.

"I am Sarah."

. "How old are you?"

"I am seventeen years," replied the girl, and asked, "Is your mother well?"

"She is well." Anna answered simply.

"Is she happy that you are a devoted thing?" Sarah wanted to know. Sarah wished she could pull the question back. How could she talk with a girl who was a devoted thing, and who was about to be offered as a sacrifice?

"She is submissive to my father's will, thank you." Anna did not want to admit that her mother was unhappy.

"It is something to think about," said the priest's daughter. "It would be a very hard thing to do, I am sure. Yet such an act of devotion must give great joy, even in the sorrow." The child was wiser than one would think.

"It is unreal and strange. There is terror, too."

"Of course, I cannot know, but I believe I would feel greatly honored. After all, to be given to God as a gift would make you very special."

"My attitude may be wrong, but I dread being burned to death. How would you feel, Sarah? Would you feel a black dread?"

"I'm sure I would, but sacrifices die very quick," Sarah observed. "Sacrifices are killed as gently as possible." (But Christ wasn't – He was abused to the limit of the soldiers' endurance.)

The girls found it very difficult to talk. The conversation was strained and meaningless.

The priest reentered the room, and sat down near Anna. He gazed at her, not knowing where to begin.

"Do you think the lambs suffer much pain when they are killed, Rabbi?" Anna asked before the man could open a conversation. "We take great care to be as kind as possible in killing the sacrifices. They are dead before the fire burns them. It is much better that they die quickly and then burned, than to be burned to death," the priest answered. "We are trained in how to sharpen the sacrificial knives, and just how to use them."

Silence fell on the room because the priest and his daughter were afraid of making Anna more apprehensive, or of causing her alarm. But after a while the priest continued.

"God Himself made the first sacrifice, you know."

"Yes, I am aware of that, but tell me again about it," Anna replied.

Sarah turned so that she could look into her father's face as the man began the lesson. "After Adam and Eve rebelled against God in the garden of Eden, they realized they were naked, so they made aprons of fig leaves to cover themselves from the sight of the LORD. God knew they would need more sturdy clothes than leaves to walk around on an earth covered with thorns and thistles; so He killed animals, and made clothes for the couple out of the skins. But the main reason God killed the animals was because the only way to atone for sin is by the shedding of innocent blood, for the life of the flesh is in the blood."

"Has a human ever been offered as a devoted thing?" Anna asked the same question her daddy had asked.

"There has never been such a thing in Israel," the priest replied, secretly thankful that he was not the one who would have to do this task.

"Do you think my father was wrong in making such a vow?" Anna asked.

"I would not judge your father, Anna. Since God made provision for making vows in His Law, then I must say that it is not wrong to make such a vow. Having made such a vow, however, it would be a grievous sin to fail to carry it out. I think a man should exercise more wisdom."

Anna looked at Sarah, and drank in the look of admiration and love for her that emanated from the ruddy face. The face was bright with purity and devotion.

"Father, let's take Anna to our scenery rock," Sarah suggested. Her eyes were bright with enthusiasm.

"Yes, I think Anna would enjoy that. We will eat supper now, and then we'll go."

"Would you like to go, Anna? We can see a great area from our tock."

"Yes, I would enjoy that, but we must take my friends." Anna brightened at the thought.

"Of course. We'll call them as we go by where they are." Sarah felt relieved that the gloom was lifting a little.

After supper Sarah, her father and older siblings struck off with Anna to the cliff. Anna's friends were collected as they went along the street. As they passed an old dilapidated building built, like the whole town, of mud bricks; Sarah informed them that this was their synagogue and school house where the boys attended the House of the Book. As they neared the cliff, they could see distant mountain tops. There was an ancient wall around the edge of the cliff to make it safer.

"You can lie across the wall, and see down to the slope below," Anna told them. One or two of her brothers and sisters were already sprawled across the wall.

"Will it fall?" Miriam asked.

"No, the wall has been there a long time. Once in a while someone jumps off the wall, and one or two have fallen off, but if you are careful, you are safe," replied the priest.

Asenath leaned over the wall, and looked down. "Oh! Judah. It's a long way down."

Anna and Deborah ran to the wall and leaned over. Miriam could hear them gasping as the sight surprised them.

"Go and look over, Miriam," urged the priest.

"Oh, no. I'm afraid," cried Miriam as she drew back further.

When Anna, Deborah, and Asenath got up from the wall, they began looking at the valley below, and a couple of miles away. They could see a city, and they began discussing whether it was be Mizpeh.

"No, it isn't Mizpeh. Mizpeh is out of sight of this place. It is to the right beyond the slope of that rises from the gorge below us," the priest told them.

Anna was disappointed that she could not see her home town. She wondered if she would be able to see it as she rose to Heaven when she died.

As the children sat of the wall facing the priest, he said, "I suppose all places like this must have their tales of tragedy. This place does, of course, and if you like I will tell it to you."

All the children agreed that the tale must be told, and the priest began, "It is told that a boy and a girl grew up in the city together, and that they learned to love each other at an early age. The girl was very fair, and the young man strong and fine. The girl's parents arranged for her to be wed to a young man in another village. The girl and boy protested, but there was a need for wealth in her family, and the young girl was worth much. All her life the girl pleaded to be given to the young boy she loved, but could not even speak to. The young boy, too, pleaded with the girl's father, but the father threatened him."

The children missed not a sound as the priest told to story. The priest continued, "At last the day came for the wedding. But the girl ran out of the house to meet the boy she loved, and they meant to run away together. Her father, however, saw her, and knew what she intended to do. He grabbed a sword, and with the help of his brothers, he chased them to this place. As the girl and boy stood on this wall, the father approached to kill the boy. Suddenly, they embraced and kissed; and with hands joined together, they leaped from the wall to the rocks below."

The children were stunned, and cried out in sorrow and protest. Miriam was horrified, and wailed.

"Did the father get her body back up?" Asenath wanted to know.

"No. Their bones are still down there, we are told."

After a short discussion, and a string of questions, the little group started back to the priest's house. The three friends returned to where they were to stay, and Anna and Sarah, with hands joined together entered Sarah's home. They slept in the same bed with another child, and early the next morning they rose up to greet the dawn. Sarah pleaded with Anna to stay with her for a few days, but Anna insisted that she must continue her mournful wandering.

Return to Wandering

Anna met her friends at the edge of the village, and the quartet went off with waves of farewell from their friends who stood in a group, and watched them out of sight. They strolled along silently until noon, when they sat down by a cool brook, and opened the bags of food that their friends in the village had prepared for them. They enjoyed the fresh food, and drank from the little stream, still without a word. As they rested in the shade of a cedar tree, Miriam at last broke the silence with the question that was hanging in the heart of all four,

"Anna, did you see what that priest did to that little lamb?"

"Miriam!" Asenath burst out, "why don't you be more careful about what you say?"

"Well, it made me sick," Miriam cried, "and I can't bear to think of what is going to happen to Anna. How will the priest kill her? Will he cut off her head?"

Anna indeed had seen what had happened to the little lamb, and she had cried about the little thing. What the priest had told her was of little comfort to her. Her heart beat rapidly as Miriam's words fell upon her ears, and she thought about having her head severed.

"It is a sickening sight, Miriam, and God intended it to be that way," Deborah said, "for a sacrifice is for sin, and sin is sickening. My father says that he will never get accustomed to killing innocent animals."

Anna sat in a painful hush during this exchange between her friends, but when they fell silent, she said,

"The priest talked to me about it last night. He told me how priests are trained to offer the sacrifices as painlessly as possible."

"My father says that when the Deliverer comes that He will bruise Satan's head: and Satan will bruise His head, and he wonders often just what that means," said Deborah.

"How did your father learn that?"

"Priests like my daddy study the Scriptures all their life, and the Scripture says,

'*And I will put enmity between thee and the woman, and between thy seed and her seed; it shall bruise thy head, and thou shalt bruise his heel.*' Genesis 3:15."

"Did God say that?" Asenath asked.

"Yes," Deborah answered.

"Who was God talking to?" Anna asked.

"He was talking to Satan just after Adam and Eve disobeyed God," I think," said Deborah.

"I don't understand the Scriptures, and I don't think anybody else does," Miriam remarked.

"Well, you may not, but there are wiser heads, you know," Deborah remarked shortly.

For two days, rain pelted the girls. They sought shelter under an overhanging rock, but soon water began running down the underside of the rock, and dripping off on them as fast as it fell from the black and gray clouds that hung just above their heads. Miriam cried and held on to Asenath, and shivered till her teeth rattled. The other three soon joined her in the soggy misery, and began to weep. Their hair was plastered to their heads and shoulders, and it seemed that all the water in Israel would fall on them during those long painful hours. During the night their affliction was almost unbearable. They could not build a fire, and their food was wet by the time they got it into their mouths. When enough morning light filtered through the clouds and rain so that they could see, Deborah said,

"We can't get any wetter by going out, so let's see if we can find a cave."

All four lasses gathered their soaked possessions, and followed Deborah out into the downpour. They stumbled along in the mud, slipping and falling again and again until at last they found a small cave. They were thankful that they had found this hole in a hill, but they hesitated. This wilderness was populated with different sorts of creatures that had sharp teeth, and a passion to survive. Some of these creatures had fangs loaded with poison. There were insects that were capable of doing serious harm to one who threatened them. One of the worst creatures to contact was the scorpion. It didn't always kill you, but it would make you hurt so bad, you'd wish you were dead. With tremulous hearts, they steeled themselves against what sorts of creatures might have taken up residence in the cave before they got there, and went in.

It was more of a hole in the hillside than a cave, and they found no creature large enough to threaten them. A few pitiful birds flew out, and a hare or two, but the girls were almost as happy with this blessed shelter as they would have been a cabin. There were even a few sticks lying around which were quickly gathered up, and set afire with a small spark created by vigorously rubbing sticks together.

After a while Miriam stopped crying; Asenath stopped grumbling, and they had some much needed lunch. They set themselves to getting dry, and in a few hours they were actually quite comfortable. They recited verses from Moses, and prayed to Elohim for protection from sickness, and gave Him thanks for His gracious blessings. Then they relaxed and enjoyed the primitive comfort of their hole in the ground.

"I feel like a little hind hunkered down in a comfy home," said Anna as she scratched mud from her legs.

"Isn't this wonderful," added Miriam, and she burst into a lilting laugh that stunned her companions, and, caused them to laugh with joy.

In fact, they were very content until the fire blazed up on a pine cone and Asenath saw a skeleton in the cave behind them, and jumped up to go see it.

"Look, a skeleton!"

All three girls quickly turned their heads toward Asenath, and when Miriam saw the skeleton, she screamed, and dashed out of the cave into the pouring rain at the speed of fear. Anna jumped up to catch her, and bring her back; and Asenath was about to follow when Deborah grabbed her and said,

"No! Stay in here out of the storm. Anna will bring her back."

It was all Anna could do to drag Miriam back into the cave, and if it had not been for the torrents that pounded their heads with icy drops: she would not have succeeded. Asenath, Deborah, and Anna worked to calm Miriam, and then they examined the bones. It was a shepherd, no doubt, because the clothes were those of a poor shepherd, but they were so decayed that it was hard to tell.

"We'll just leave him alone, and he'll leave us alone," Anna said: and all four went back to their fire, where Anna and Miriam dried out. They were not as comfortable as before, however, and hoped the rain would soon pass. Suddenly, an enormous head filled the entrance of

54

their cave, and all four girls jumped up screaming, and ran in terror for the back of their hole. The head disappeared as quickly as did the girls, and they saw the huge animal stop a hundred feet from them, and turn around to look at them. There were two other great creatures, and all three stood in the rain looking at the girls in the cave.

"They're behemoths," laughed Deborah, "as harmless as lambs. We probably scared them worse than they scared us."

"My daddy says they are very gentle," Miriam added from her place behind Asenath.

"Well, let's go get one, and make a pet out of it," laughed Anna.

The big animals meandered off into the rain carrying their twenty-foot tails behind them.

Anna began having nightmares of lambs being slaughtered, and frequently she would cry out: and Deborah would come to hold her, and comfort her as she wept herself back to sleep.

One day they approached some shepherds to ask for food, but the men were rough, uncouth individuals who had no respect for young women in a wilderness. They chased the girls, but the girls were so fleet of foot that they outdistanced all but one of the men: and he overtook Miriam, and dragged her to the ground. The other three girls hurried back to rescue her, and pelted the man with stones until he was well bruised. Loudly he screamed curses at them, and ran for his life. The girls could have run with him, and beaten him to the ground, but they let him go.

"What a rascal," Anna growled. "Are you all right, Miriam?"

"Yes, but, oh, I have a thorn in my foot," she groaned as she pulled off her sandal. She was surprised at how dirty and callused her foot was.

"I'll never get the dirt off me when I get home," she whined.

"Let me look at it," Deborah said, dropping to her knees.

Miriam sat quietly while Deborah searched for the thorn in the sole of the grimy foot. The other two girls sat gazing into the distance. At last, Deborah found the thorn, and having no fingernails, she pulled it out with her teeth.

"Ugh," she gagged, spitting profusely. When her mouth felt clean, she said, "your foot may get very sore, Miriam. We may do less walking for a few days."

"I'm tired of walking anyway," remarked Asenath to herself.

The girls sat in weary stillness while the sun blazed down on their itching heads. This was homesick time.

"I think your father is a fool!" Asenath ejaculated angrily.

The other two girls jerked their heads around toward her, but they only gazed at her in disbelief that she would express what was the secret opinion of all three of them.

Then Deborah rebuked her. "You are a hysterical woman, Asenath! Calm yourself, and remember that we are here to mourn the fate of our sister, Anna."

"No," Anna said calmly, "she has only spoken what many people have in their heart. And she is my friend concerned about me." Anna put her arms around Asenath.

Asenath leaned against Anna, and lifted her voice in wailing. Anna cried also; but she patted her friend gently, and said, "A man can do foolish things, my dear, and yet not be a fool!"

Asenath was sorry she had hurt Anna's feelings, but she had started something that she was not going to stop until she had cleared the air, and clearing the air was one of the reasons for their journey, she concluded.

"What did he expect to come out of his house first that he could have offered to the LORD as a burnt offering, anyway? Do you keep sheep in your house?" She asked, striving not to be too impudent.

Anna was surprised that Asenath made the same remark that her mother had made to her father. "We have all conceded that it was a rash, foolish vow, but one foolish vow does not make a man a fool," Anna insisted.

"But, Anna, you are so good, and sweet, and precious to everybody. How can it be right to destroy you?" Miriam was wailing again.

"I don't believe I am being destroyed. If I believed that, then I would have some serious problems. I am being given as a gift to God. I can only get out of my body to go to Heaven by being killed. Death seems terrible, and it is, but for me, it is like flying out a window to meet God just outside. No one can judge my father but the LORD our God. My father has done something that has bound him in a dilemma. To offer me will hurt him and my mother, but if he does not pay his vow, then he has played the fool in the eyes of God. People often do things that make it impossible for them to do right without sometimes hurting other people. My father is trusting God to make a way of escape if it is not His will for him to do this."

"But anybody ought to know that it would be worse to kill you than to break a vow. Isn't murder worse than breaking a vow?" Asenath demanded.

"You cannot say that, Asenath, because you don't know. It cannot be murder to do something that is clearly demanded by the Law of God. It cannot be wrong to obey the Law of God. My father would gladly die before he would harm me. And he does consider me more important than any ordinary vow. God does not want a sacrifice that doesn't cost us something. But this vow devoted me to God. He gave me to God. God gave my father a great victory after he made this vow: and my father loves God even more than he loves me. I would have it no other way. God could have saved my life by not granting my father the victory." Anna was comforted by her own reasoning, and her companions found it difficult to counter her argument.

"Perhaps a defeat for Israel would have thwarted God's plans for something else," Miriam interjected. "After all the Messiah must come through Israel, and the seed of Juda must be preserved."

"God is sovereign and His plans for mankind cannot be thwarted, Miriam," Anna answered. "But it is a matter we shall never understand in this world. My father loves me, I know that, and his suffering is greater than mine. I die on that altar only once, but my father must live with his memories and die many times. The pain in my heart is for my father, for he is the one who made the vow;"

"How does it feel to be most holy to the LORD, Anna?" Miriam asked.

"It is a sensation of bright purity, Miriam. I no longer desire to remain on Earth. I am happy about the prospect of seeing Paradise. I feel that God is so pleased with me."

"Your mother must be very angry toward your father," Asenath observed.

"My mother's suffering is very great, but she is submissive to my father's will. She knows his frailties and sympathizes with him: but she knows that he is a man of great integrity and faith. She knows that he must pay his vow," Anna answered.

The girls sat pensively looking down into the plain below them while ravens squawked in the distance.

"Does our Law provide for a female being offered as a sacrifice?" asked Asenath.

"I don't know," Anna said, her brow furrowed with concentration. "As far as I know, Scriptures command us to offer male calves and bulls and rams for sacrifices."

"Look at the vultures circling over there," Deborah remarked, pointing into the blue sky.

An Encounter with Cats

The girls were drawn in that direction because they had nothing to draw them in any other direction, and almost before they knew it: they had gotten within plain sight of two lions devouring an animal they had killed. In terror, they dropped to the ground behind a rock, too scared to make a sound other than gasping for breath. Anna raised her head above the rock, and watched the big cats tear the animal apart.

"Do we run, or what?" whispered Miriam through white lips.

All the girls were stiff with fright, and nodding their heads, "No!"

Anna felt a finger prodding her arm, and when she turned her head, she saw a great lion with a massive black mane meandering slowly toward them. They were trapped between the big lion and the two that were eating the animal! Anna flattened herself on top of the other three girls as they lay as close to the earth as they could get. She could hear the heart beats of the others, and wondered if the cats could hear.

Anna hoped the big cat would see them, and kill her, and free her poor father from his terrible task. As she watched the great beast coming closer, she resolved to jump up and run so that she could lead him away from her fellows. She prepared herself for the leap, but she felt a tug on her hair as Deborah took a handful of it to hold her down. Deborah perceived what was in Anna's heart, and took away her option. Suicide was not an acceptable solution for her daddy's dilemma. The lion's eyes were fastened on the other two lions, and he was within a few cubits of the girls when he suddenly sprang forward to attack the two lions that were feasting. He went by the girls so close they could hear his breath.

A vicious fight ensued, and the girls jumped up and ran for their lives. They stumbled and ran, holding each other up, dragging each other, picking each other up, frantic flight and safety for all four their only thoughts. They ran until they were completely spent, and collapsed to the stony ground to pant like hares that had been chased by hounds.

"That, my dears, could only have been a miracle," Deborah said, when she had caught breath enough to gasp the words. "The LORD God refused to allow His devoted thing to be torn by an animal,"

Asenath agreed. A gaze lingered between Deborah and Anna that spoke plainly, for Anna knew that it was Deborah who held her when she was ready to fly into the jaws of the lion. They understood each other, and did not discuss what was in their hearts.

"We cannot know how many times God has spared us in this wilderness because of the precious devoted thing we are in the company of," Miriam, said.

"I always dreamed of having many children," said Anna, after they had rested a while. She looked far into the distance as if she could see them there. "My mother told me often that she had wanted many children also, but God allowed her only me. I know my father wanted a son very badly, but I know I am as precious to him as a son could ever have been."

The Ruins

As they wandered aimlessly along in silence, they found themselves near some ruined houses. The ancient houses were barely recognizable with only a few walls standing more than three feet high. Curiously, the inspected the ruins, and soon realized that the old village was the home of ancient Canaanites. Others had been there before them, so the clay bricks were scattered about, and nothing of value remaining. As the girls looked over the place, one turned over a crumbling cornerstone of a house, and exclaimed,

"Look, everybody!"

The girls gathered around, and saw a tiny bone protruding out of the stony dust.

"Is it something they ate?" asked Deborah.

"I feel a sense of evil," shuddered Miriam.

Anna stooped, and raked the dust and pebbles back. More bones were uncovered, and a tiny skull.

"I think I know what this is," shuddered Deborah. "My daddy told me that the Canaanites worship Ba'al.'

"I remember, too," said Anna, "in the days of the great Judge Gideon, the Midianites invaded Israel. God commanded Gideon to cut down their grove, and throw down the idol Ba'al." (Judges 6).

"Many Israelites worshiped Ba'al, too." Deborah agreed. "Ba'al was worshiped by burning their babies alive. When they dedicated their houses, they would put the burned remains of their first born son in a jug, and seal it in the cornerstone of their house. That must be what this is."

By now both Miriam and Asenath were bawling.

Anna ran her fingers through the sand again, and a small brass image appeared.

Deborah screamed, "Oh! That's an image of Ba'al! Don't touch it! We must flee from the evil place. Run for your lives!"

She was twenty feet away, running as fast as she could run. Anna jumped erect, and followed Miriam and Asenath as they fled in terror from the ghostly place. One of Asenath's sandals flew off, and missed Anna by only a few inches. She stopped and grabbed it, and overtook Asenath limping toward a flat rock. Quickly, Anna put the sandal on the dirty foot as Asenath leaned back, and held her foot high. They resumed their flight, and soon overtook Miriam and Deborah. Exhausted at last, the girls fell to the dry ground, and panted.

Dusk Talk

"Aren't you scared, Anna?" asked Miriam.

Anna sat in mute anxiety; tears streaming down her sun burned face. She shuddered to think of the searing flames of the altar fire, and the awful dagger that would end here life.

"Just think how many poor lambs and calves have been offered as burnt offerings," she whispered. "Man's sins have caused much suffering in the world."

"Your father will have to offer another sacrifice after he offers you," Deborah observed.

"My father will offer a sacrifice, but not because he sinned by offering me," Anna replied, "for he made a vow, and he is bound by the Law of God to keep it, and a man cannot sin when he is obeying the Law of the LORD."

"I have never been able to understand why God makes us do such awful things," Miriam sniffed.

"It is because man does such awful things, Miriam," Deborah said, "and God would rather have an animal die than for a man to die. Justice is not easy to understand or live by. Sin is death, and God must impress that upon man." She was only a child, but her spiritual understanding was not shallow.

"It is God's will that man live righteously before Him. Righteousness brings joy and peace into our lives. But when we are foolish and wicked, then God's justice demands retribution. A sacrifice atones for our sins, and that shows us how awful our sins are," Anna explained

"One thing is certain for me: I will never do anything without praying about it, and being certain that God wants me to do it," Miriam resolved.

The quartet agreed that they had learned that lesson. "My father says that God will send a Deliverer Who will put an end to all these sacrifices, because somehow the Redeemer will be sacrificed. It is all very hard to understand," Deborah said.

The girls did not fully understand because *the* LORD Jesus Christ would not be born for more than a thousand years after they lived, and much Scripture about the coming Redeemer had not yet been written, but all the sacrifices they offered were pointing to Jesus Who would die on an altar that was a cross. The cross would stand on Mount Calvary which was virtually no more than a heap of earth and uncut stones.

(That would happen no more than thirty miles from where they sat. His blood, shed on that cross, would show us how terrible our sins are, and when we receive Him as our Savior, His blood will cleanse us from every sin. And He would be the last sacrifice ever accepted by God for man's sins; He would be the perfect Sacrifice. Offering animals for sacrifice after Jesus died is just a cruel waste; for the veil of the temple was rent down, opening the way to God for all who would come with Messiah's blood. Even offering our works as a sacrifice is a waste of time: God will not accept them any more than He accepted Cain's. Jesus Christ is the total Sacrifice.)

"Come now, and let us reason together, saith the LORD: though your sins be as scarlet, they shall be as white as snow; though they be red like crimson, they shall be as wool." Isaiah 1:18.

"Anna," Deborah said, her girlish curiosity at last overwhelming her reticence to break the subject, "who did you wish to marry?"

Anna bit her lip for a few seconds, and then allowed the tears to streak down her face again, while she rocked back and forth on the stony earth. This was the most bitter thing she had to accept: she would never marry. She had wept a flood of tears since coming up on this mountain, and there seemed no end in sight for her, for the face of the one she had secretly chosen was ever before her now. Her three fellows, too, lifted up their voices, and added their tears of sympathy and personal woe, for this matter opened again the reason for their being on this mountain. Deborah put her arms around Anna, and their tears streamed down together. Every time they entered this area of thought, they went through this same agonizing, exhausting ritual.

"You know the one I hoped my father would betroth me to," Anna sniffed. "He with the broad shoulders and sharp wit. He who was always first to help when there was someone in need. He who loves the Scriptures, and spends extra hours memorizing them. I had hoped and prayed that my father would arrange for him to have me to wife. Our children would have been strong and fine. I had even hoped that Eve's Seed would have been borne of me."

The afternoon melted away, and the sun was nearing the horizon before their emotions dried up, and they could cry no more. Their weeping seemed to be coming to an end.

"I wonder how Anna got along today," murmured her mother, as she sat at the table, a plate of untouched food before her. Tamar appeared many years older than she did the last time we saw her. There seems to be a lack of life about her. Her hair seems grayer, and her face more wrinkled.

"The damsel is strong. She is like her father and her mother," replied Jephthah evenly. He had not inherited anything from his father: his father had never shown him any affection or support, and his life had been bitter in exile. He had surrounded himself with bad companions, and their influence on him had made him a rash and reckless fellow, but he was a fierce fighter, and a good leader; and through it all he had great faith in God.

Now he was perplexed and suffering great consternation. He had made a vow unto the LORD his God, and

"If a man vow a vow unto the LORD, or swear an oath to bind his soul with a bond; he shall not break his word, he shall do according to all that proceedeth out of his mouth." Numbers 30:2.

Why a faithful man like Jephthah would make a vow that bound his soul, without prayer and thought, we can never know. But men are prone to do rash things, on occasion.

Jephthah was not blessed with the Holy Spirit's leading as we are today. Mistakes were much easier to make. The war he was facing with the Ammonites was so important that he was willing to give anything for the victory, and anything was what it cost him: his precious daughter. God is cruel to hold a man to such a vow, some would say. No, God is not the God of people whose word is of no value. God said,

"When thou shalt vow a vow unto the LORD thy God, thou shalt not slack to pay it: for the LORD thy God will surely require it of thee; and it would be sin in thee."

All who knew him had pleaded with him to break his vow, but he was inflexible in his determination to honor God by honoring his vow.

"I cannot bear it," groaned the wife and mother.

"You can bear it, and you will bear it," Jephthah replied resolutely but tenderly, "a man who breaks his vow is a fool in God's sight."

Ecclesiastes 5:4 would not be written for more than a hundred years after Jephthah died, but he knew it to be a truth.

"A man who makes a vow without much thought is a worse fool," replied his wife curtly, as she left the room.

Jephthah gazed at his partially emptied plate, his hands motionless, as he admitted to himself that she was telling the truth. He had been a fool to make a vow, especially such a vow as he had made, without thinking about it carefully. But now as he turned the facts over in his mind, he believed that he had done the right thing. Many lives had been saved, all of them sons of fathers like himself. Perhaps the entire nation had been saved. Jephthah knew that through Israel the promised Deliverer would come. But, oh, if it only would not hurt so badly. The food he had eaten lay heavily on his stomach, and his heart throbbed with dread.

On the Mountain

Anna awoke before dawn on that last day. It had been exactly two months since she left home, and today was the day she must return. Her hair and bed cover were wet with dew, and her teeth rattled in the predawn chill. She backed close to Deborah who lay beside her. Dread lay cold and heavy upon her heart as she considered this, the last full day of her young life. She knew her father well, with his faults and all, but she loved and honored him nonetheless. He would answer to God for his actions, just as she would. She prayed that God would be merciful to him, and her mother, and to her.

A bird chirped in a nearby bush, and Anna reluctantly opened her eyes to see the faint rosiness of dawn. She arose and slipped on her sandals, and quietly tiptoed across the gravelly ground to a rock where she knelt to pray. God touched her heart and gave her the peace, courage, and strength she needed. She felt close to Paradise. She would soon be there. She and her companions had spent two long months on this wild mountain, bewailing her coming death as a young woman who had never had the joy of being married and knowing a husband. The girls were worn thin, physically and emotionally, and now the time was at hand to end the journey. She said a detached good bye to him with the broad shoulders, and turned her attention to Heaven.

Mrs. Jephthah and Keturah

Tamar had not wanted to see the dawn. Her fitful sleep was laced with prayers for her death. Anything would be better than life as it was for her now. The dread of the coming death of her daughter was a pain that extended from her heart into every fiber of her being. She dabbed her face with water; numbly dressed herself, and strapped on her sandals. She went to her kitchen where she met her servants and instructed them for the day. Then she went out the back door and across the yard to a tiny cottage in a corner of the wall. This was the home of ancient Keturah who had raised her and her mother. Mrs. Jephthah's grandfather had brought Keturah back from faraway Midian when she was only a tot. She was such a delightful little thing that many of Gideon's warriors had wanted her, but Mrs. Jephthah's grandfather received her as a gift from Gideon for his valor in battle. Keturah was now blind, and spent her days sitting before her tiny fire place warming her wrinkled hands.

Jephthah had retired her to this comfortable little cottage, and given her servants of her own. They were preparing the old woman's breakfast when Mrs. Jephthah entered the little room. Mrs. Jephthah knew that she had waited too long to come here. She would have gained much strength and wisdom weeks ago if she had come; but she dreaded what the old woman would say to her. She knew, actually, and did not want to hear it, but now she must.

Though a Midianite, Keturah had long ago believed in the God of Abraham, Isaac, and Jacob, and grown to be a woman of great wisdom and understanding. She was a counselor to many women in Mizpeh and the surrounding area; and now her mistress needed her more than them all. Mrs. Jephthah affectionately hugged the aged one, and sat down on a stool beside her.

"I'm sure you have heard the sad news, Keturah," she began.

"I have heard," replied the old lady with a surprisingly strong, clear voice in spite of the absence of her teeth, "but I am not so sure it is sad news."

"You aren't!" exclaimed Mrs. Jephthah. Tamar knew the old lady would say this.

"No, my dear. Anna is now a devoted thing, and what greater honor for a person than to be a devoted thing, most holy unto the LORD?" replied Keturah with breathless wonder.

"But she is my only child, Mother, and she is going to die," ejaculated Mrs. Jephthah. "I will have no child: I will have no grandchildren."

"You will have your child. She will be in Heaven instead of here."

Mrs. Jephthah began to weep again. "I hoped at least you would understand."

The two young ladies who were Keturah's servants were very much attuned to exchanges such as this, but they went on with their work as if they did not know anyone was in the room.

"I do understand, my dear, it is you who does not seem to understand," said the old woman gently, touching the silver streaked hair on the head of her mistress. She remembered caressing that head when it was first born. There were deep lines of worry across the face of the mistress, and her countenance was gray and downcast.

"Explain to me," Tamar wept.

"Hebrew women are rarely named in our Hebrew Scriptures. The wife of Noah must have been a giant among humans, but we do not know her name. Shem's wife was the mother of half the world's people; but we do not know her name. Judah and Levi had wives, but we do not know their names. We do know Joseph's wife's name, I am glad to say, for I bear Joseph's name. Captain Joshua had a wife, but we do not know her name. But I can assure you that they are known to God."

"Anna's name may never appear in the holy Scriptures, but you may be sure it will be known to God. Your name will be known to God because you are her mother, and you will give her to Him."

Mrs. Jephthah stopped her sniffing, and wiped her face, and looked into the aged, angelic face.

"There is no greater gift to give than your child. There is no greater joy than giving the most precious thing you have to the one you love the most. If you love the Receiver of your gift, then there will be joy in the giving of the gift, and the more you love the gift, and the more you love the Receiver of your gift, the greater the joy in giving."

Mrs. Jephthah stared into the clear, black eyes of her servant. She knew all this: she just needed the strength to accept it.

"But a gift can be given only out of a willing heart," continued the counselor. "If you give Anna instead of having her taken from you, then you will have joy to undergird you in your sorrow and loss. Don't be afraid

"What time I am afraid, I will trust in thee. In God I will praise his word, in God I have put my trust; I will not fear what flesh can do unto me." (Psalm 56:3-4).

"But I do not have the option of giving. She is being taken from me by my husband," Mrs. Jephthah objected.

"But, my dear, you do have an option. If you give the child, then your husband cannot take her. One cannot take what he has been given: he can only accept it."

"If he offers her, he will have to take her from me because I do not think he did the right thing, and I will not give her," Mrs. Jephthah decided.

Anna's Peace

Anna returned to the camp where she leaned some dry sticks against each other, and blew the embers until the fire blazed up. Anna sat and watched the birth of the new day, and pondered Paradise, and all the saints who were there.

Twelve centuries later, Jesus would tell the story of a poor beggar who would die, and find himself in Abraham's bosom being comforted, but Anna did not have that reassuring knowledge. Besides, she would not go to Paradise, but to Heaven, for God was waiting for His devoted thing.

Physically she felt very old; her long black hair seemed gray, and her smooth face seemed wrinkled and dry. Death should come only for the aged. Spiritually she felt an eternal spring blooming in her soul. She looked forward now to her death as a relief from remorse and regret, and felt closer to Heaven than to Earth. She was resigned. Serenity flooded her soul, and her fears vanished. A celestial joy and peace came over her that was almost too heavy for her mortal flesh to bear. She experienced a comfort of body and spirit that took away all sense of time and age. She sensed an eternal glow in her being. She was now oriented to Heaven and eternity, and Earth and its inhabitants, and its time, were foreign to her. Her exhaustion vanished. Her face became smooth and radiant. She hardly felt the pull of gravity. Anna's companions awoke, stretching themselves after they sat up, shivering to hasten the flow of warming blood through their bodies. After nibbling a few bites of dry bread, and drinking some tepid water from a goatskin bag, they knelt quietly to worship their LORD. It was only then that the girls noticed Anna's appearance.

"Anna! Your face is radiant and clear. You're beautiful!"

There followed minutes of rejoicing and embracing. Still on their knees, they praised the God of Israel: the God of Anna. Presently they rose, and started down the mountain toward Mizpah, and the altar. They held hands as they went, their dirty clothes dragging tatters: their matted hair too heavy to float on the morning breeze. There was no girlish giggling, no youthful chatter. It was a procession of victory.

But Miriam could not continue long without weeping and talking. "Anna, why don't you flee to a foreign land?" She stopped and threw her arms around Anna.

"Oh, foolish woman," Anna scolded, "you who called my father foolish. I would meet a fate worse than death if I did such a thing. I am submissive to my father, and to my God. Does not our law command us to honor our father and mother?"

"I think a parent who makes such a foolish vow is not honorable," Miriam retorted.

Anna would have been justified in being very angry at her young friend, but she had become so removed from the world, that anger was not possible for her.

"If there is one thing certain upon the earth, it is the fact that no one is perfect. God said Job was perfect, but then Job had to repent. My father is but a frail man, as all fathers are, but he is my father and he loves the God of his fathers. That entitles him to my love and obedience."

"That same Law promises that '... ***thy days shall be long upon the earth*'," instructed Miriam.

"I leave that in the hands of the Lawgiver," replied Anna, with an angelic smile brightening her face. "I will obey."

"Now Miriam, stop this rattling, and rejoice with us," commanded Deborah.

The four friends had shed so many tears that it seemed there could be no more, but as they embraced, there was a new overflowing, and their embraces left each other dampened with drops of joy. This parting was very sweet, and there was hope that they would all meet again in a better place and time. Anna's friends hugged her as if she were some sort of angelic creature. Though held in their arms, she seemed far removed from them. At last the farewells had done all they could, and each walked away in her own direction.

It was late evening when she arrived at her front door. Timidly, she knocked, and when the door opened, she fell into the arms of her mother. When she stood back minutes later, she could not believe her eyes.

"Oh, Mother, what has happened to you?" she cried.

"I gave myself to our great God last night, my dear, and after that it was easier for me to give you to Him, too. I surrendered it all last night. I know your father is right, and we have given ourselves and you to the God of Abraham, Isaac, and Jacob, our fathers," her mother replied calmly.

When Anna first saw her father come through the door, his haggard face revealed the misery that had been his companion since he arrived home from the battlefield, but now as she looked at him, his countenance was bright with joy and paternal affection.

The family sat quietly together before the fire all night, murmuring encouragement to one another, and talking of things precious to them. One parent would hold Anna for a while, and then the other. They talked of heroes of long ago; the prophets and priests who walked with God, and whose lives were examples for them to live by. They also talked of people who failed in their obligations to God, and upon whom God inflicted great punishment. They even remembered Adam and Eve; and how God had kept His word to them. They remembered a number of their ancestors who had suffered horrible fates because they disobeyed God. They recalled Achan and his stolen wedges of gold and fine garments that he hid under his tent. They talked about Judah's two wicked sons whom God slew. Even sons of Aaron and Eli, high priests of Israel, fell under the wrath of God.

The presence of Jehovah in their home that night was very real to the little family of three. The peace of God that passes understanding so strengthened them that they were able to discuss the past two months, and confess how difficult it had been for them to reach to point of total surrender to God. Mrs. Jephthah related how that she had gone to old Keturah for sympathy and solace, and came away with a heart filled with conviction. She told them about giving the most precious gift to the dearest friend. Anna was the most precious gift she could give, and God was her dearest friend.

Jephthah told his family that he was filled with peace when he saw the face of Anna when she returned home. Though he saw the same facial features, there was something that he perceived to be holiness within her that radiated through her face. That radiance made him know that she was absolutely a devoted thing most holy to the LORD.

Anna told her parents that she had resolved the matter when she realized that God could create other worlds, and take whatever from them He wanted. But there was only one Anna, daughter of Jephthah, and the only thing God would take from her was what she gave Him. His love for her constrained her to love Him, and yield to Him all her heart, and all her soul; and all her mind, for though she was giving her body to be burned, without love, it would profit her nothing.

Before dawn began to lighten the sky, the trio rose and went forth into the darkness toward the field which Jephthah had purchased for the purpose, and where he had erected an altar of uncut stones. On the top was piled dry sticks for a fire to consume the sacrifice. As they approached, a glimmer of light from the eastern sky revealed the dark figure of the priest standing by the altar. Anna trembled with an indescribable ecstasy, and her parents felt a peace that passed understanding. With hands shaking, and eyes blind with tears, Jephthah wound a cord around his daughter, and lifted her and laid her gently on the wood.

He took from its sheath a knife with newly honed blade, and struggling to maintain his balance, handed it to the priest. The priest took the knife and raised it above the still, virgin body of Jephthah's precious daughter.

Suddenly, there appeared above the altar an Angel of magnificent countenance: light radiating from His being as if electricity flowed through Him. Jephthah and his wife staggered back in terror, and the priest fell to the ground, quaking with fear; but the Angel said,

"Fear not, Jephthah, for thy daughter is a devoted thing, most holy unto the LORD."

Then the Angel put forth the staff which was in His hand, and touched Anna, and there rose up fire out of the altar; and fire engulfed her, and she and the Angel went up to Heaven in the flame.

Please take note of Judges 6:21.

"Then the angel of the LORD put forth the end of the staff that was in his hand and touched the flesh and the unleavened cakes; and there rose up fire out of the rock, and consumed the flesh and the unleavened cakes. Then the angel of the ORDL departed out of his sight."

Gideon offered to the LORD an offering, and this is the way that God showed His acceptance of it, and how He took it. Evidently, this is the same way God took His devoted things, such as Jephthah's daughter.

Jephthah continued to serve the LORD after his daughter was offered, and God gave him great victories over his enemies. He served as judge of Israel for six years, and was buried in one of the cities of Gilead.

Epilogue

Jephthah was a man of faith and courage as seen in his unyielding devotion to the Law, and its Giver. His character and courage are seen because he kept the vow which he had vowed. This reveals the enormous power of the life and work of Jesus Christ Who delivered us from the curse of the Law. In three short years of ministry, and His death, burial, and resurrection, Jesus changed a people who had lived for fifteen centuries under a system of unyielding law strictly enforced to the sort of people we see in the New Testament who were called "Christians," and the church today. In three years, Christ made a total change in the religious beliefs and practices of Israel, and virtually the whole world. The Apostle Paul is a stunning example of this great power to change. He was instantly changed from a perfect example of Law to a perfect example of Grace. Jephthah and his family lived under the burden of the Law, yet their faith in God's grace is an example that must encourage all of us.

The Golden Altar

Of the labor of my hands
Can fulfill The Law's demands;
These for sin could not atone;
Thou must save, and Thou alone:
In my hand no price I bring,
Simply to Thy cross I cling.

"Rock of Ages, Cleft for Me."

Augustus M. Toplady,
1740-1778

The Golden Altar

AM I GOING TO HEAVEN WHEN I DIE?

"Am I saved?" is a legitimate question for every person who professes to be a Christian to ask himself. In fact, that is what the Bible tells us to do. Remember, Jesus said,

"Not every one that saith unto me, Lord, Lord, shall enter into the kingdom of heaven; but he that doeth the will of my Father which is in heaven." (Matthew 7:21).

Everybody who says he is saved – isn't. Simple faith alone in Jesus Christ saves, but it also changes.

It is wise, therefore, to heed the admonition of II Corinthians 13:5, which says,

"Examine yourselves, whether ye be in the faith; prove your own selves. Know ye not your own selves, how that Jesus Christ is in you, except ye be reprobates?" (II Corinthians 13:5).

Are you a reprobate? How can you know? Here are some suggestions to get you started examining yourself. Remember, be honest with yourself.

1. "Do I love the Lord Jesus Christ with all my heart? Do I live like it?" Matthew 22:37

2. "Do I love to read His love letter to me (Bible)?" John 17:17; Psalms 119:11

3. "Do I love to talk to Him (pray)?" I Thessalonians 5:17

4. "Do I love God's church, and desire to be with God's people to worship Him?" Hebrews 10:25

5. "Do I confess my sins to God, or just rationalize them away (make excuses)?" I John 1:9

Only God can know, and only you can be sure you are saved. Are you? You must face this question sooner or later. Will you go to Heaven, or Hell? The choice is yours. Almost as important is this question: "Do I want to live in joy with Christ, or in vain with Satan? There are only two choices. They are yours to make.

The Golden Altar

Cain was happy: tired, but happy. His tomato vines were loaded with luscious fruit, and his entire garden was like a basket summer fruits. His hands were hard with labor. He was barefoot; stripped down to his waist; his tunic covered with dirt and small clods. His coal-black hair was matted with sweat. He was hot from exertion, but the canopy God had placed overhead on the second day of creation filtered the rays of the sun, and allowed only the soft, salubrious rays to reach Earth. Cain was tall and muscular. Cain worked hard on his gardens and every year he had enough produce for the whole family. Cain was the first-born. The first human ever born, and his parents, Adam and Eve, took special pride in him.

His father was somewhat angry at God because God had cast him out of the garden of Eden, and even though God had forgiven him for his sin, Adam was still agitated about being cast out of the garden. God had killed animals in place of Adam and Eve, and had clothed them with the skins. God ordered Adam out of the garden; Adam would not go. God then sent angels to cast him out, and there was a violent scuffle as Adam resisted the angels. But the angels prevailed, and Adam and Eve found themselves thrown through the eastern gate into a cursed world never to enter the garden again. Paradise on Earth had ended for them (Genesis 3:23, 24).

Cain was very meticulous with his gardens. With great effort he kept the thorns and thistles out, and each row had to be straight and clean. The rich virgin soil brought forth plants that were strong and healthy. Insects were a problem, but the air was filled with birds that ate them. The air was pure and sweet to the nose. The soil was watered by a mist that came up at night while Cain and his family were asleep in their snug, mud brick home.

He wiggled his toes in the rich black soil, and went back to work, chopping weeds out of the long rows with a hoe he had made of iron in his metal-working shop where he smelted ores. As he labored, he remembered the conversation he had had with his younger brother, Abel. They had met at the river where Abel was watering his flock of sheep.

"Cain," Abel had said, "an Angel of the LORD our God appeared to me a while ago, and told me to write down certain instructions for an offering He wants us to make at the end of shearing season." The boys spoke the original Hebrew language.

"Again? You said an Angel appeared to you once before and gave you the story of creation," Cain answered.

"Yes, He did, and this was the same Angel. I believe it is Jehovah Himself," replied the younger man. He leaned on his staff, and thought about the experience with delight.

"So what did He tell you?" Cain was skeptical.

"Here, it is all written down," replied Abel, handing Cain a rolled up scroll.

Cain read the neatly written scroll, and handed it back to his younger brother. "I have no sin I need to repent of," he said, "God surely means for other people who don't obey Him to offer a lamb." His sarcastic tone was not missed by Abel..

"But, Cain," Abel replied, "God makes it absolutely plain that all men everywhere must repent, and offer a sacrifice."

"Well, I'll have to see what Father thinks about it," Cain answered.

"I will show this message to Father as soon as I can see him."

"Well, you show your message to Father, and we'll see what he has to say about it. I'm going to get Lela and Dinah to help me gather my squash," Cain said over his shoulder. Some men are more interested in squash than sacrifices.

Abel, too, was a large man, standing nearly nine feet tall. His skin was brawny, but not sunburned. He spent most of his time in the sun, but the filtered sunlight did not burn. He was greatly concerned about Cain, as well as his father, because they seemed to harbor a resentment against God for expelling their father and mother from the garden. The angel with the flaming sword at the eastern gate was a Spartan reminder every day of that terrible event (Genesis 3:24).

A wolf came down to the river's edge, and finding a place among the drinking sheep, quenched his thirst in the cool, clear water of the river

Hiddekel. There were animals of different sorts cavorting in and along the river and its banks: a great dinosaur grazed on the water lilies which grew again almost as fast as they were devoured; beavers frolicked in and out of the water; eagles flew overhead: all was calm and serene. No creature was a threat to another. That would come later.

Abel picked up a little lamb, and led his flock to a new grazing spot. He sat down under a tree near a soft meadow. He took out the scroll that contained the sacred words, and looked at it very carefully. He had put down every word, just as the Angel had uttered them. He had prepared his pen of iron to take down the words of the Angel when He appeared, and to record interesting events as they occurred. He read the words again, which gave detailed instructions as to how God wanted the offering made. God would never commit His commands to word-of-mouth or to any group of people because He would hold everyone accountable for what he did with the commands. These commands were very simple. Man was to build an altar of rough stones and earth (Exodus 20:24, 25), and place a large pile of dry sticks on top. The most perfect lamb was to be chosen from the flock and beheaded, and its little body laid on top of the wood, and fire set to it. This would create a hideous sight, but it would be a perfect picture of man's sins; and, after all, all men have sins (Romans 3:23). To Abel it seemed altogether reasonable and rational to make an offering such as God demanded.

But Abel was puzzled. Why would God require the offering to be made on an altar of rocks and earth? Plain rocks that had not been chiseled in any way would be unattractive. It would not seem a worthy sacrifice to the LORD God the King of Glory. He looked at the parchment again to be sure he had understood it correctly. It was there in black and white. He wondered if God had built an altar of uncut stones and earth when He killed the animals for his parents' sin in the garden (Genesis 3:21).

Cain stopped to wipe the sweat from his face, and take a long drink from his goatskin bag. His sisters, Lela and Dinah were laboring beside him in other rows. Cain had decided that he would take Dinah for his wife. Jehovah had not handed down laws against incest, and it was only natural and right that men marry their sisters. The gene pool was still perfect, so perfect children would be born of such unions. He decided that Abel was just mistaken about what he thought Jehovah had said. That business about an altar of earth and stones was doubtless wrong. God would want a beautiful altar, one of gold and precious stones. Cain knew that God had spoken to Abel before, because Adam had read what Abel had written, and verified that what Adam knew of creation was set down accurately by Abel. Also, the life of Abel was testimony to his relationship to God. But it didn't really matter whether Elohim had spoken to Abel or not, Cain made up his mind in a flash that God deserved better, and that he would provide it.

Cain also decided that he would ask Dinah that very day if she would be his wife. He made good on that resolve that evening after they had eaten in the family dining room. His approach to Dinah was not very romantic. He simply asked her if she would be his wife, and she consented. There was nothing she could do but marry one of her brothers if she was to have children, and she had an irresistible desire to be a mother like her own mother. She was a beautiful woman; tall and slender, with black hair down to her waist. Dinah wore a linen garment from her neck down to her knees. She was not quite as beautiful as her mother, but she was nearly perfect; the first girl born on the earth. But the men did not seem to notice the beauty of the women; that was just the way they were. He took her by the hand and they went into the sitting room where Adam was resting from his labors, and told him they wanted to be married.

Adam stood before the couple and told them to join their hands. Then, remembering the words spoken by the Creator in the garden of Eden when He joined him and Eve together in holy matrimony, and witnessed by the rest of the family; Adam joined his two children together for life as husband and wife. After the brief ceremony, Cain took his bride to the cottage he had built for them a short distance away.

Adam was working hard in his mine. The minerals he was digging for were not very far below the ground, but he had to find an outcropping of them, and begin digging. Sometimes, Eve would help him, but more often he would work alone. He dug for gold most of the time, but he also dug iron and copper and zinc which he mixed together to make brass. All of these metals were valuable to him, but he loved gold particularly because it was easily worked into beautiful things. He made dishes of it, arm bands, bracelets, and necklaces: he even tried to make a house of gold but it collapsed, and he was fortunate to get out of the rubble alive. Of gold, he made a full sized golden statue of a lamb for Abel, and all sorts of vegetables and fruits for Cain. Adam loved gold so much he could hardly think of anything else. He would melt it over and over again to make it more pure, and then make blocks of it for later use. He was very near to the point of making gold his god. He'd do anything for the soft, lovely metal.

"Dinah, are you sure you can make a tall, pointed hat the way I want it?" Cain asked his wife. "It must have much gold and jewels on it."

"Yes, but I will have to get your father to make a frame for it. Just how much weight can you carry on your head?"

"I can carry much weight, but don't you worry about that. You be concerned about how beautiful it is," answered Cain, swelling with pride in his strength.

"How tall should it be, Cain?"

"It must be about so tall," Cain answered, holding one hand about four feet above the other.

"Well, that will require a heavy frame."

"Now, for my shoes," Cain went on. "They must be of the finest lambskin, with jewels and precious stones. I will ask Abel to make them for me. He will ask much broccoli for them, but whatever the cost, I will pay. As for my robe, Lela, I want you to get Dinah to help with it. It's the most important part."

"All right," answered the sister-in-law who had been called in for the planning session. "Shall we make it of silk?"

"Yes, but I want it made of special silk. Every worm must be specially chosen, and they must be fed only the choicest tea leaves."

"But, Cain, there won't be time to produce silk from the worms," it was his wife. "We must use what we have."

"Ummm." Cain cursed under his breath. "I hadn't thought of that. Well, anyway, choose the finest silk, and use it. The LORD will just have to be satisfied with the best I can do." Cain rubbed the hair on his face while looking at Lela. For the first time in his life, he noticed how pretty Lela was. Why in the world hadn't he chosen Lela instead of Dinah? "My robe must have lavish decorations on it," he went on. "I am making an emblem to wear around my neck, with beads for me to count in my spare time."

"You plan to do this in a big way, don't you?" said Dinah.

"Of course, I must do my best for Jehovah. I am now designing the altar," he went on, while fondling a golden pear that Adam had made. "It will be twenty cubits long and eight cubits high, and I'm going to gold plate it. Then I'm going to put huge piles of the most beautiful produce I can find on tables on top of it. "

"Oh, Cain, that will be lovely!" exclaimed Lela. Cain licked his lips.

"Nothing is too good for Jehovah." He swelled with pride.

"He should be proud of you," Lela interjected. Maybe ...

They worked until the night was far spent, and then straggled off to their bedrooms. The evening mist had risen, and nothing stirred outside. There were no night creatures to sing or prowl about in the mist, and so the night was silent except for a very slight murmur of the air. Their cottage was very comfortable. Adam and Eve had lived in a cave until they learned to make metal tools, and then they were able to build houses of mud bricks. Their beds were comfortable, too. They had learned that it was much better to sleep above the floor than on it.

Lela lay in her bed and stared at the blackness above her. She wondered how much longer it would be before Abel asked her to get married. He seemed very happy that Cain and Dinah had gotten married. But she couldn't be sure that Abel would be interested in marrying at all. The whole family knew he was a prophet, more interested in angelic visits than anything else. He spent a great deal of time praying.

Eve was always the first to get up in the morning. She cried for weeks after she enticed her husband to eat the forbidden fruit, causing God to cast them out of the garden (Genesis 3:6), but her beauty was still intact. Adam wouldn't get up until she had breakfast prepared, but when he got up, he was always in a great hurry to get into his day's work. Eve worked with swift efficiency. Eggs were broken into a golden bowl, and fruit was cut up with a silver knife. She sliced bread and smeared it with butter.

Abel woke up in his tent, pitched near to his sheep. There were no predators: but he had to tend them because they were so dumb they would walk off a cliff. He knelt to pray, and stayed on his knees for several minutes. He was not interested in gold or produce: or even sheep, but Jehovah alone. He poked around in the fireplace until he had a blaze, then put it to work cooking his breakfast. Eggs and oat meal. He thought about the coming offering, and realized that he would have to choose the most perfect lamb in his flock to be killed and offered. His father and brother would also need lambs to offer. It would be a great day.

Cain came across the meadow, and Abel rose up to meet him when he got closer.

"Good morning, Brother Cain, how are you this fine day."

"I have never felt better," Cain was exuberant.

"Wonderful," shouted Abel. "Have a cup of tea." He poured a cup of tea into a golden cup Adam had made for him.

"Good. I will." Cain sat down by the fire and took the cup he was offered. "Abel, I want you to make me a pair of shoes for the offering. They must be of the finest leather, and covered with bells. I will pay you well."

"Oh, I don't know," Abel replied cautiously. "Why do you need bells?"

"Abel, I've decided to offer God a beautiful offering. I have the women even now working on my new garments. They will be the finest material, covered with many precious stones. Oh! How fine I'll look. I've picked out a perfect hill top where I will build my altar, and it will be overlaid with pure gold and precious stones. I will engrave many angels on it, and God's hands receiving my gifts (Exodus 20:4). It's going to be twenty cubits long, eighteen cubits wide, and ten cubits high. It will be piled high with all sorts of different fruit and vegetables that I grow with my own hands. Only the most perfect will do. I will be dressed in my new garb, and I will march around it, and on it with certain icons I will make. God will be so pleased with my hard works." (Titus 3:5)

Abel heard all this with a frown on his handsome brow. "Cain, you must not do that. God made it very plain in His word how we should give our offerings. God said to offer a lamb on a heap of uncut stones and earth. We should dress in our finest, but to dress up like you've described is not necessary: or acceptable."

Cain was angry. His heart blazed with rage. He dashed the cup of tea into the fire, and rose to his feet. "How dare you presume to tell me how to worship God?" he snarled. "You have your religion, and I have mine. I don't believe in bloody religions or a bloody God. I have not sinned, and I do not need to offer a lamb."

Abel got to his feet also, and looked straight into Cain's eyes. Abel was angry at Cain's foolishness, but worked hard to conceal it. "I did not call myself to be a prophet. Jehovah called me while I was among the sheep. He spoke to me clearly, not only once, but two times, as you well know. He told me to write the words which I did, and I showed you a copy. It is not what we can do for God, but what He can do for us that matters."

Cain was enraged. "You think you have a lock on what God says. You think you are the only one who knows anything about God. Well, I'm telling you that I will worship God as I please, and He will be happy to take what I give Him."

"We please God by faith, and His grace takes away our sins. I was moved to write the words of God, and you will be wise to heed them. Elohim will not accept your offering," Abel said to him with finality in his voice. Cain clenched his fists and gnashed his teeth. He kicked Abel's little fire, scattering sparks and cooking utensils over a ten-foot circle.

"Speak to me of this no more," he growled as he walked away.

B y early afternoon Cain had the framework of his altar completed. He looked with great satisfaction at the freshly cut and hewn timbers. He decided that he was not as good a carpenter as he was a farmer, but he was happy with himself. Then he thought of Abel's words. The very idea of Abel preaching at him! Who did he think he was anyway – God Almighty? He got angry all over again. *I'm as good as he is any day of the week.* Cain's thoughts went on and on while he rested in the deep shade of a poplar tree.

He had asked Adam to help him, but Adam told him he was too busy with mining to waste time building an altar. Adam could never have a right relationship with God as long as he harbored resentment in his heart toward God. Adam would sell Cain the gold and precious stones he needed for his altar; and that was as close to it as he wanted to be. Adam had a good store of food on hand, but he would accept some more. Cain would pay him whatever he demanded. Adam had been told by the LORD that he was to eat bread by the sweat of his brow, but Adam had decided that he would rather eat Cain's bread, and use his sweat to dig for precious minerals and stones. God would have to be reasonable if He wanted Adam's respect.

Cain had sawed a tree half in two, and now he used it to pour molten gold from an iron pot on it to cool into a solid. As it cooled, he beat it into a thin sheet, which he nailed to the framework of his altar. The sheets of gold were very heavy and hard for one man to manage, but Cain doggedly kept on until he had several sheets fixed to the altar with nails of brass. He fell in exhaustion, and lay for several minutes while he caught his breath.

The sun was almost gone when Cain got up and started for his cottage. He could hardly put one foot before the other: totally exhausted. He arrived at his door staggering so that his alarmed wife ran out to meet him and help him to the table. She paid little attention to the flecks of gold and silver on his clothes. His wife wiped his blazing face and arms with a damp cloth. Dinah put his food on the table, and asked him how his altar was coming along. He told her he was completely pleased with it, but he would have to hurry if he finished it by the day of the offering. Cain was ravenous, but he had to pay attention to what he was doing to stay awake. At last, when he had eaten his fill, Dinah helped him to his bed where he fell without taking off his clothes. A couple of hours later, he woke up and put on his night clothes.

Adam put the last bar of gold on his two-wheel cart, and commanded his donkey to pull it. He was going to the location of Cain's altar. Adam had learned a long time ago that donkeys were obstinate, but obedient creatures. The concept of the wheel was vaguely in his mind from the day he was created, and it did not take him long to develop it.

The journey was not long, but required a couple of hours for the never-in-a-hurry donkey. Adam had also learned that the donkey would travel at its own speed wherever it went, and whatever the circumstances. The cart was quite heavy, for gold, after all, is heavy metal, and Adam didn't want to spend much time in the business of delivering it. He carried a sack of precious stones from his storehouse, which Cain had ordered. He would return with his cart loaded with vegetables from Cain's gardens. Food lasted a long time in the pure air beneath the canopy.

Cain's huge body was wet with sweat when Adam approached. "Hello, my father," he called. "Are you well?"

"Oh, yes, son Cain, and are you?" Adam dropped the reins of the little animal, and wiped his sweaty face with his sleeve. He took a few more steps toward his eldest son.

"Yes, all is going well today. Father, as you know, Abel has been saying some very troubling things to me."

"Yes, I know." Adam's face darkened as he nodded his head, and dropped his eyes.

"He told me that you deliberately disobeyed God when you ate the forbidden fruit."

"That is true, Cain. I did not do a good job of explaining to your Mother exactly what God told me about the tree of knowledge. After she ate it, I didn't have much choice."

"What did God tell you?"

"Well, I've told you before. Actually, it was a very simple, reasonable command. He told me not to eat any fruit from that tree."

"But why? It seems so foolish: unnecessary."

"It was not foolish. The Creator has the power and the right to do whatever He pleases, and everything He pleases is good. Before I ate the fruit, I did not know I could kill Eve if I wanted to. I did not know I could lie to her; steal from her. I was innocent of these things before. Now I am evil, for I am capable of doing evil."

"But it's not fair for Abel and me to be evil just because you are. Why couldn't we be innocent like you were?"

"A good thing cannot come out of an evil thing, my son. When you plant wheat, you get wheat. When you plant potatoes, you get potatoes. You came out of me, so you are what I am."

"Well, I will do right. I will be good. I will offer God my best fruits."

"Didn't Abel tell you that offering your fruits is wrong - evil?"

"Yes, but who is Abel? Just a religious fanatic."

"Better offer a lamb, like God said. Some day He will send a Lamb to die for all of us."

"I'll offer Him my fruits. God will balance my good against my bad. Besides, I like doing religious things."

"You better do what God says." Adam felt like a hypocrite.

Why should I? You don't."

"Well, that's different. I just don't have time for all that. Anyway, you've been told," said Adam, looking at the massive gold box his son was constructing. "Three or four more days and you will finish the gold plating. Where will you put the jewels?"

"Oh, I will form them like animals. I think that would be best, don't you? Maybe I will make a couple of images like the angels with the flaming swords at the garden gate."

Adam picked up the reins, and drove the cart nearer Cain's furnace, and more closely examined the altar. "This gold is heavy, Cain. I hope your frame will hold it all."

"It will, Father. I was careful to put in plenty of wood at the right places."

"Well, we must not waste too much time talking. Do you have payment ready?" Adam would not trust anybody; all of whom were members of his own family.

"Yes, Father, it is in these boxes I have stacked here," replied the younger man. Cain had to be part carpenter because he had to make crates for his produce. Adam looked at the fruit through the slats of the crates, carefully counting the crates as he went. Produce was almost as valuable as precious metals and stones. After all, you could eat produce whereas precious metals and stones were only things of beauty to admire.

"If you will help me unload the gold, I will help you load the produce," Adam said, being careful to keep the trade as nearly even as possible, their labor being of great value to each man.

"I wish we had Abel and the women here to help. The stuff is really heavy," Adam remarked as he picked up one of the gold bars. They worked silently after that, conserving their breath and with it, their energy, and soon had the cart unloaded and the produce loaded. The job was done quickly for both Cain and Adam were big men, with powerful arms and shoulders. Adam gave the donkey a slap on the rump, and they started for Adam's barn where he stacked his produce in a cool, shady corner. He looked at the stacks with satisfaction. He thought he would have to tear down his barns and build bigger ones. He repeated the thought to Eve later that evening, and she aggravated him when she said,

"Why do we need bigger barns, Adam? There's only the two of us here in the house with little Mary." Mary was only two years old.

"We may have needs in the future, Woman. And besides, food is money, and you can't have too much of that."

"But God will supply our needs, Adam."

Her husband was surly. "Maybe. I'm not taking any chances. God said I would eat bread by the sweat of my brow, and that is what I'm doing."

"But you know that God intended for you to till the soil," replied Eve.

"Don't lecture me, Woman. You've no right to tell me what to do," Adam snapped back, and with finality in his voice.

While Cain was working to the limit of his strength, Abel was quietly leaning on his staff watching his sheep. He saw the beauty of God's creation, and communed with the Creator. As he walked among the sheep, he watched for signs of injury. There was virtually no sickness, and insects were harmless to animals, as all other creatures were. Occasionally, he had to kill a sheep, for the hides were of value for making clothes and tents. He never thought of eating a sheep.

God had not yet permitted the eating of flesh. Sheep and people were different sorts of creatures, because God had breathed into man the breath of life. Their bodies had been made from the dust of the earth, and in that they were alike, but the spirit made men different. Man lived by the breath of God.

Often, Able would stop and sing a song that was composed in his mind as he meditated. The songs he sang were of creation and the goodness of God. He would sing of God's victories over Satan and his angels, and of God's awesome power. Often, Lela would come out to the pasture where he was and they would spend hours talking. Lela, like Abel, was very devout, so the two of them talked much about creation, and the things God did for their parents in the garden of Eden. They were sorry that their parents had disobeyed God, and wondered what life would have been like in the garden. The angels were still there at the eastern gate with their flaming sword, and would remain on guard until the flood hundreds of years later.

"Cain's robe is fabulous," said Lela. "It is heavily embroidered with gold thread, and it is covered with precious stones. Cain will not be able to wear it very long at a time because it is so heavy."

"I am very concerned about Cain. He doesn't seem to care what God says, but rather decides for himself how he will worship. It's as if the words of God are not written down. And he won't pay any attention to me."

"Well, Dinah is content to do what he says. She doesn't seem to have an opinion," Lela remarked. "Cain is working himself almost to death to get everything prepared for the sacrifice. He is not able even to thank God for his food before he eats."

"I told him that his works are not pleasing to God, but he keeps on. It's like he is driven by some demon. When he's working all the time, he doesn't have time for God."

"It's better to obey than sacrifice," said Lela, quoting a prophet that would be born centuries later. Then changing the subject, she said, "Cain and Dinah had a beautiful wedding, didn't they?"

"Yes, I guess Father remembered the words of the Creator when he and Mother were married in the garden. That was surely a beautiful ceremony, too," Abel said, thinking now would be a good time for him and Lela to be married.

"There were no witnesses to their marriage, except the animals," remarked Lela wistfully, thinking that now would be a good time for Abel to ask her to marry him.

"Lela," Abel began, "you and I have the same mother and the same father, but I - I have a strange feeling for you. It's different from the feeling I have for Mother and Dinah. I have a desire to be with you all the time. I would like very much to be married to you. Will you agree?"

"Of course, if Father will approve and do the ceremony like he did for Cain and Dinah. They both live now in Cain's house. I could live in your tent."

"Would you like that?" Abel asked.

"Yes, I would." Lela radiated the glow of joy.

"Then let's pray and ask Jehovah if it would please Him if we become husband and wife." Pause. "I'll build you a house."

The matter was now settled between Abel and Lela, and they hoped Adam would agree.

"Father," said Abel after supper, "Lela and I have talked and prayed about getting married, if you approve."

"Well, how can I disapprove, since you are the only marriageable man on Earth, and Lela is the only woman on the earth who is not married, and the Creator commanded us to be fruitful?"

"You will marry us, then?" Abel wanted to be sure.

"Are you and Lela ready?"

"Yes," replied Abel with pulse racing. "Let's do it tomorrow night. What do you say, Lela?"

"That's wonderful, Abel. I'm quite happy."

"All right, we'll do it tomorrow night," said Adam.

There was no such thing as incest in those earliest days, for God intended that the world be populated, and there were only brothers and sisters at the first. Incest was not wrong until God said that it was wrong hundreds of years later in His law (.See Leviticus 18). Fourteen hundred ninety years after creation, man had become weaker because of the second law thermodynamics, and his genes had become much weaker, too, so that near kin would possibly bring forth sickly children. But in those early days, there was no problem of childbearing for brothers and sisters. Eve and Dinah were happy when they were told of the coming wedding. Poor Cain was at home in the bed, twisting in an exhausted sleep, with bed sheets wrapped around him. Eve, in her quiet, unassuming way, kissed her daughter, and blessed her

Y ou are working too hard, Cain," said his adoring wife as they rested a few minutes, "why don't you slow down a little bit?"

"Get behind me, Woman, you know I can't rest when the day of the offering is so near," growled Cain with voice full of anger. It was not just exhaustion that drove him to be unkind, it was his ungodly nature. Unbelief kindles wrath.

Dinah sniffed a little bit, but Cain was untouched by her tears. "You don't love me."

"Love you, shmove you. What do you expect?"

"Just a little kindness and affection."

"Are you sure you have my robe completely done?"

"Yes. You can look at it any time and see, but I can't think of anything else to do to it."

Cain got up and strode off to closer inspect his almost-finished altar. Lifting the heavy, awkward sheets of gold and nailing them in place had taken much strenuous work, but Cain was satisfied. The great golden box glittered in the early afternoon sun; the object of Cain's affection. Dinah walked up beside him, and said,

"It is so beautiful, Cain, I love it. You have done so well."

"In the afternoon before the sacrifice, I must gather fruits and vegetables of all sorts to pile upon my altar, I must gather the finest stuff I have grown, and arrange it all in perfect order. The different colors must harmonize so the LORD will be pleased."

"He will have to be pleased after you have worked so hard."

"Abel's idea about offering to God an altar of earth and stone does not apply to me. I've been too good, and done too many good things for God," Cain said vehemently.

97

"You surely have," his wife agreed.

"I've got my religion, and he's got his. He can worship his way and I'll worship my way. Everybody ought to love each other, and try to get along. A man can have too much religion anyway."

"That's for sure."

"In fact," continued Cain, "I think you should dance around my altar, too."

"Say, that's a great idea."

Cain had to stop talking while he manhandled the final sheet of gold into place. He put his shoulder against it to hold it while he nailed it. He had many a cut and bruise where he had been nicked by the gold plates, and hit by falling objects. There was no need for a scaffold because Cain could easily reach ten feet to the top of the altar and still nail.

"Now," he puffed, "for the decorations. I need all the golden fruits that Father made for me, and a few more, too. I brought what I had from the house this morning in the cart."

"Oh, Cain, don't get carried away," warned Dinah. "I think it's pretty enough."

"Don't worry. I am still going to own all this. I'll just have it here. I'll tear the thing down, and reclaim my gold."

"Well, we don't have to give too much."

"I can even get more. After all, Father must eat." Cain thought that was very funny, and roared an echoing laugh. "And Abel, too." The laughter got louder. "Golden ears of corn in the shuck on the corners there would look good." His mood changed very quickly from laughter to serious thought.

"Some silver sheaves of wheat would look good, too," added Dinah.

She had deep, troubling doubts about all religious roads leading to Heaven,

"Oh, yes. But I'm almost exhausted now," answered Cain as he slumped to the ground. His face glowed crimson red, and his mouth was dry.

"Cain," exclaimed his wife, "you are working yourself sick!"

"I just need to rest a few minutes."

"You've been working every day: not even taking off the seventh day to rest, as God commanded," said Dinah.

Cain rested for a few minutes while he surveyed the surrounding countryside. It was a lovely place. You could see for miles. It was the highest hill anywhere nearby so you could see over the small hills. All the mountains were low hills covered with pasture land or trees. Off to the west he could see the garden of Eden with the angels faithfully standing guard at the gate. No one could enter the garden now; it was forbidden territory. He could not discern the tree of life or the tree of knowledge of good and evil, but he knew they were in there somewhere. The impassable wall stretched on for miles around the garden. The rivers that flowed out of the garden sparkled in the late afternoon sun. Fish jumped and skittered about on the surface of the water, and alligators and hippopotami wallowed. Eagles and falcons gorged themselves on berries and nuts just as modern parrots do, leaving the squirrels and rabbits to scamper about without a care. Camels and lions grazed the tall, nourishing grass, each with jaws much alike.

"I believe I will build an altar ten feet high on top of this altar, and this altar will become the platform for the smaller altar. Since it will be smaller, I can pile it high with chosen fruits," said Cain as he sipped cool water from a brass cup.

"But, dear, won't you run out of time?" objected his wife.

"And think of all the work you'll have to do."

"I think I can do it, and remember, I'm doing this work for God," Cain answered, his voice choking off as he swelled with pride and emotion. but she kept her t

"Maybe God doesn't want you to work for Him. Did He call you to do this? Look all around you – everything you see is the work of God's lips," Dinah told him.

"Be quiet, Woman, I won't hear any more of that sort of talk from you!" Cain shouted.

Cain began furiously working on the altar that was to top his original altar. He had the framework up by nightfall, and the next morning was busy again working as fast as he could. He had to make smaller plates of gold now to cover his altar, and the wiggling sheets were almost impossible to carry up the steps, but he persevered, thinking how God would be pleased with his efforts.

Abel was busy watching butterflies landing on his knees and exploring him with their proboscises. Birds flocked around him and chattered noisily. Other animals would come to visit during the day: leopards, hyenas, wild goats, gazelles, panthers: all sorts of creatures. Often a calf from his herd would come near to be petted or scratched. The cows did not graze with the sheep because the sheep ate the grass so close to the ground, but they got along well together, and stayed close. Snakes were the only creatures that stayed away. Abel would see one once in a while skittering along the ground where God put them, but they were not a threat to him. An irrevocable curse is a horrible thing. As bad to contemplate as Hell itself.

He spent a lot of time that day thinking about the marriage that was planned for the evening. He thought about the future, and how the world might be in, say, a hundred years. There would be many little children, for God had specifically commanded them to have lots of children. Eve was still having children, and Dinah would bring forth little ones, and Lela, too, would bear young: his young. He couldn't think much further ahead than that. He didn't want to. Today was a day unto itself. He stroked the feathers of a bird he took off his shoulder, and was amazed by the beauty of it, and the perfect shape of its feathers. He looked carefully at its beak, and wondered that the Creator could make such an instrument. He bowed his head and said,

"I thank You, O Jehovah, my Creator, my God, for the work You have done. With the breath of Your lips, You did create us, and with the skill of Your hands have made us."

The prayer was not long, but as he was constantly amazed by the things about him that God had made, he prayed often. He prayed for Lela that God would bless her with many children, and long life. He prayed for his father, that Adam would develop a right attitude toward God before he died. He prayed for the whole family.

It was late in the afternoon when Able decided to drive his cows, and lead his sheep back to the corral he had built near his tent. He had to prevent their wandering at night so he could sleep.

He went into his tent home, and thought of how good it would be to have Lela waiting on him when he came home at night. He must begin building her house as soon as the offering was done. He wanted to show her the frog eggs in the river's edge, the birds' eggs in the trees, and the flowers that grew everywhere. They had plenty of time to see God's creation.

Abel chose his best clothes: clothes he had made of silk threads he had spun while tending his flocks. It was easy to take the raw silk off the worms, and then spin it between his fingers. He put his robe on over his tunic, and after a quick stroke through his hair with his iron comb, he was ready.

It was different for Lela. She felt a desire to be elegant, and she did her utmost to be just that. She washed herself in plain water, and then covered herself with olive oil she had beaten out. Crushing olives in an iron pan with a brass bar was hard work, but it was well worth it. Her perfumes were made of different plants, and mingled perfectly with her body to make the perfect aroma. She went into the kitchen and offered to help Eve with the supper preparations, but Eve would not permit her to remain in the kitchen very long. This was Lela's big night, and certainly she shouldn't have to work in the kitchen. In spite of her exquisite beauty which no woman could match, Eve was a sad, melancholy person, always blaming herself for the fall in the garden which led to their expulsion. No one could ever convince her otherwise.

Lela went into the other room, and found little Mary playing on the floor with her little toys.

"Hello, Mary," she said, delighted to see her little sister.

"Hewo," was the little girl's reply. She was happy to see Lela, too.

She gurgled and laughed as Lela played with her on the floor. Lela loved children, and hoped she would have several. Dinah came into the room, and sat down beside Lela. Dinah also felt the love of motherhood as she held Mary in her arms.

"Where's Cain?" asked Lela.

"He fell asleep while he was eating supper," Dinah said.

"You mean he won't be here to stand beside Abel?" Lela asked.

"No, he was just too exhausted," Dinah said, and then in an effort to change the subject, she said, "You are so beautiful, Lela."

"Thank you, dear I wanted to look my best. I'm so sorry Cain was not able to come."

The girls played with little Mary until Eve had the meal on the table and then they all feasted: except poor Cain who was in his bed exhausted, too tired even to take time to thank God for the day. Abel and Lela then stood before Adam while he said a few words binding the young couple together as long as they both lived. Joining a brother and sister together as husband and wife was especially beautiful, and could only be done in those early generations. It was a joyous time for all of them. They skipped around the room, clapping their hands and singing songs they made up as they went. But Dina's joy was darkened by her husband's absence.

Cain didn't pray that morning because he was hurrying to finish his altar. He was eager to get to the site of his altar and work on it today. He didn't think of Abel and his bride, to offer his congratulations or anything. He could think only of his altar and how good he was to build it for God. He failed even to realize that his gardens were getting weedy. But the great altar stood there in the bright morning sun, gleaming in all its beauty – the emblem of how much Cain was willing to do for God. How little faith he had in God's grace. As he put the last brass nail into the last strip of beaten gold, his heart nearly burst with pride. It was about that time that Dinah arrived.

"Oh! My dear, how beautiful your work is," she exclaimed, wishing she could feel good about it.

"Hurry, we must get the area cleared of all this rubble," Cain told her as he began to load his cart with the tools he had been working with. Dinah worked beside him, picking up small pieces of wood and metal that he had dropped.

"Now," he said, wiping his fevered brow, "you finish up here for me, while I go to my gardens. They must be grown up by now."

"All right," she answered, "I'll be down there as soon as this place is clean."

Cain drove his donkey before him as he hurried to his little barn. He unloaded his tools and threw out the trash, and headed for his gardens, never a minute of rest. His garden was full of weeds, but he soon had many of them cut down. He had built a small shed near his gardens in which he kept his garden tools. He had an iron-headed hoe which Adam had made for him, and several other things. Soon Dinah joined him, chopping furiously.

"Let's begin picking fruit, now, Dinah. I don't want to get caught by the night."

Without a word his wife put away her hoe and did as her husband said. They loaded the cart with the fruits, and then took them to the altar. When Cain came down the steps the last time, it was late evening, and he could barely see. When he got home, he was almost too tired to eat, but Dinah faithfully set the table with good things: beans, corn, potatoes, and the like, and he ate without prayer or thought of God's blessings through the day. He was thinking of his altar.

The next morning, Abel and Lela walked toward the golden altar sitting on its hill several miles away. When they came within a half mile of it, they could plainly see it flashing sunshine all over the landscape.

When they got closer, Abel stopped to gaze at it in admiration. "It's extraordinary," he murmured.

Long minutes passed before either of them spoke. Dinah appeared in the clearing and greeted them.

"Good morning. Cain will be along shortly," she said cheerily.

Abel knew that all of this work was in vain, but he greeted Dinah cordially.

"How much of this did you do?"

"Very little," Dinah admitted. "It was Cain's project from start to finish."

"But how did he put that gold on?"

"He just manhandled it all the way."

"It's no wonder he's been so tired."

The trio sat down under a great chestnut tree near the altar and waited for the arrival of Cain. Then, after waiting awhile, Dinah got up and said, "I'd better go and see if I can help him."

"We'll wait for you here," Abel called after her.

103

Dinah raced through the trees on a path that led to her home. She was almost to the house when she met Cain, puffing up the hill.

"Dinah, I can't make this collar stand up the way it should," he said, turning around so she could see.

Dinah worked for a several minutes on the wayward collar before she succeeded in fixing it.

"Now, you run ahead and let the others know that I'm coming," he said with an air of superiority.

Dinah again did her husband's bidding without a word. When she arrived at the place under the chestnut, she found Abel and Lela quietly talking about how lovely it was on this hill top.

"Cain will be along in a few minutes. His robe is very heavy," she told them, "and besides that, he has on a tall hat and is walking with a very heavy staff."

"He'll be along soon, and we're in no hurry. The sheep and cattle will be scattered some, but we can round them up easily enough."

Dinah sat down, and in a few minutes' Cain came out of the woods, seeing no one, but waving his hand around as if he were surrounded by a great crowd. Abel and the two wives got up and went near to the altar nervously, afraid they would do something wrong. Cain went to the foot of the steps, and knelt for a while in a posture of prayer, then he arose and lit the candles in the lamp he had made. Then he rose to his feet and went up the steps chanting something no one could understand. At the top of the steps, he knelt again in lit incense in small brass pots, and stood again before his offering.   "God, I thank You that I am not as other men are: extortioners, unjust. I fast twice in the week, I give of all that I possess. This offering and all my perfect fruit I give to thee."

Nothing happened. The heavens were silent. Cain expected God to do something. He repeated his prayer.

ABSOLUTELY Nothing.

Cain expected an angel of the LORD to appear. There was nothing.

He stood there. Nothing. He repeated his prayer again.

At long last he came down from his great altar, taking off his hat as he came down the steps.

"I don't understand," he said. "There was no response from Elohim."

Abel did not want to comment. He knew why God did not accept Cain's offering.

"It's all right, Honey," Dinah said, "God had to be pleased with your altar and your offering."

"It is a beautiful altar, Cain," said Abel, thinking he was safe in saying that. "Come let's go offer my offering."

"No, I must go home to take off this robe; it's too heavy to wear to your place. I'll be over there as soon as I can change."

"All right, I'll wait," Abel replied.

Dinah was troubled by the whole situation. Was Abel right when he said God demanded a plain altar and a lamb? Why? She was badly confused. Could her husband be wrong? No. But that was only the opinion of a faithful wife.

A s soon as Cain changed, he and Dinah went to the place of Abel's altar where he was about to offer the little animal, kept up for several days for testing before the offering. Abel had piled up a heap of stones, and while the three others watched, he severed the head.

"LORD God, be merciful to me. a sinner," he sobbed while the little bleeding body was still in his hands. He laid the carcass and the head with all the fat on the top of the pile of sticks. Abel then knelt with the women and cried while the fire burned. Cain remained standing, and watched with contempt.

As the four of them watched, an Angel appeared above the altar, and said that the God of Heaven had accepted the offering. Then He touched the offering with the tip of His staff, and a flame rose out of the altar and consumed the animal. The Angel, without another word, disappeared into the blue sky.

Cain was thunderstruck! An Angel of the LORD accepted this hideous pile of stones and dirt, with a dead, bleeding animal on it, while his gorgeous altar of such hard labor was ignored and lay yonder on a hilltop with now rotting fruit on it. He had worked so hard, paid so much
—

Slowly Cain turned and left. He walked off into the woods toward his house. Dinah followed him, weeping for what had happened, and what would happen. She felt so small and helpless tagging along behind her husband. Works and faith contrasted.

When Cain arrived at home, he went to the table and sat down. His anger was slowly rising as he thought of the recent events. He knew that God had killed animals and made clothes for his parents, but he felt like this was different. His parents had sinned. Cain didn't seem to realize it, but they had deliberately disobeyed God's command, just like he had done. There was no excuse for them doing that. His mother had listened to the serpent, and eaten the fruit without talking to his father about it. What could his father do, he reasoned. With his wife condemned, his father had no choice but to eat the fruit. Cain felt that God was entirely unreasonable, and his anger continued to rise.

Dinah came in and sat down beside him.

"Darling, I would not worry about it if I were you. You'll find that God loves you just as much as Abel," she consoled.

Cain cursed under his breath, and mumbled something Dinah could not understand. *Abel was out there in his poverty, living without a care in the world, while he and his father worked their fingers to the bone, and who does God appreciate? You'd think there was some virtue in being poor. Abel earned virtually nothing with his beloved animals, but he was God's favorite,* Cain decided. His gorgeous, gracious wife sitting beside him seemed to mean nothing to him. She did her best to get his attention to convince him to reconsider, and listen to Abel, but Cain ignored her. Cain had thrown his costly robe to the floor, along with the staff, hat, shoes, and trumpet, so he was sitting there with nothing on but his tunic. Dinah finally got up, and went about picking up the expensive clothes, and tenderly cleaning them and putting them away. Cain continued to curse and smolder.

The next morning, Cain went to his altar to tear it down, and reclaim the gold and other valuables. When he arrived, he was stunned to see that it had collapsed into a broken heap. All his labor had collapsed because it did not have a good foundation. There's no foundation without faith. He became angrier and angrier as he thought about the situation. And then Jehovah spoke:

"And the LORD said unto Cain, Why art thou wroth? and why is thy countenance fallen? If thou doest well, shalt thou not be accepted? and if thou doest not well, sin lieth at the door. And unto thee shall be his desire, and thou shalt rule over him." (Genesis 4:6, 7).

Cain fell backward when he heard the voice. He lay on the ground thinking of what God had said, and decided that if God couldn't accept his beautiful altar, then He wouldn't accept one at all. The sin God spoke of, lay at the door until Cain invited it in, and Cain found himself in an almost uncontrollable rage. He looked toward heaven and shook his fists, and through clenched teeth cursed God. He went to his tool shed, and grabbed his mattock. There was no tree of life here for Abel to flee to, so he would fix Mr. Abel. It was God Who was actually the object of his murderous intentions, but he couldn't kill God.

With boiling blood, Cain strode off to where Abel was watching his animals.

"You think your religion is better than anyone else's," he said to Abel. "You think you know all about truth. You think no one else's beliefs matter. You caused God to be angry with me."

"I do know the truth, and you could, too, if you'd obey what God has said. God has made it clear that He will do the work and we are to rest in it. God wants us to rest in His love."

"You self righteous fool. You think you know it all, but everybody is entitled to believe what he wants to. It's a free world, and I have my rights." Cain was dangerous.

"You do have rights. You have the same rights I have, and those rights are provided by God."

"Why are you so narrow minded and intolerant? Our father is not like that."

"I am intolerant because God is. God gave only one way to please Him. The only way to go to Heaven is to obey God."

Cain knew he was losing this argument: he didn't have a leg to stand on, but he was mad with rage, and he thought he had all the answers. He did not have an authority he could quote, or a rationale that would hold up under scrutiny.

"How do I know the words on that paper are the words God spoke? I just have your words for it. Maybe you changed them, or put them down wrong."

"In the final analysis, you know they are the words of God because He speaks to your heart through them." How did Abel know that God had spoken to Cain? Did Abel know that God had spoken audibly to Cain this very day? Nothing makes a man madder than engaging in a losing religious argument, and Cain certainly was losing this one. All humans of all time would lose religious arguments when they take the position that their religion is as good as anybody's, or they are good enough to go to Heaven the way they are.

Cain drew himself up with pride. "Well, God will weigh all my good works and all my bad works in a scale, and I'm confident that my good works will outweigh my bad works,"

"That's not what God said," Abel replied.

"You're always telling me what God said," shouted Cain, his rage at a white-hot heat, "you're not the only one that knows what God says."

Cain swung the mattock in his hand, and struck Abel in the head. Abel was dead before he touched the ground, but Cain continued to strike his dead body until it was a mass of bloody tissue. Swinging the mattock felt good, and Cain looked around for more victims. One of Abel's favorite calves was standing near, and Cain killed it with a vicious swing of the mattock. He continued his killing spree through the herds and flocks until the remaining animals at last ran off in terror.

Cain looked around at the bloody scene, and felt like a giant – an evil giant – and he liked the feeling. He could kill anything but God, and if he could get God in range, he would kill Him. His clothes and his hands and face were bloody. Abel's life – his blood – was crying to the LORD for justice, but Cain was unaware of that as he gazed at the result of his madness. He threw down his mattock, and strode off toward home. When he arrived there, Dinah was cleaning the house, but she stopped suddenly when he appeared, and she cried out,

"Cain! What happened?"

Cain fell on a chair with an attitude of a troubled man. "I took the life out of Abel. He wouldn't leave me alone about religion."

Dinah staggered back in shock, trying to absorb her husband's words.

"You took the life out of him? Do you mean you shed his blood?"

"Yes, that's what I did."

"Then he deserved it," Dinah declared, always the faithful wife, but so rattled she didn't know what she was saying.

"But what will Father and Mother think?" Cain cried.

"What will God think?" asked Dinah in horror.

Lela was happy with her new tent home. She hummed as she busied herself about the place, making it more livable. Birds were singing along with her, and small animals grazed around the place. The gate of the sheep fold was open, the way Abel always left it so he could get the sheep back in at even. She had practically forgotten that Abel was her brother; he was her husband now, and she loved him with all her heart. They thoroughly loved life together, constantly talking about something. She was only sixty years old, and Abel was older, but their ages did not mean much when people lived nearly a thousand years. She had a brass pot of beans cooking just outside the tent over the open fire, and she went out to check on them. She wanted to have them done for Abel's lunch. She would take them out to the pasture where he was in a short while. A lion came near to her, and she scratched his ears, and spoke kind words to him, and sent him on his way. His great jaws were green from eating plants.

At last, Lela had Abel's lunch ready. And she started off on the path that led through a clump of trees to the pasture. She sang lovely hymns about creation as she went, being careful all the while not to spill the lunch. The trees were teeming with small animals, and the squirrels came down to bark at her as she passed. The world was such a beautiful place, she thought, even under the curse. She came out of the forest on a low hill, and she could see Abel lying on the ground in the distance with a few sheep and cattle lying with him. The sight was rather odd, and Lela, who had lived without fear all her life, suddenly felt uneasy.

As she got nearer to Abel, she became alarmed because he didn't move, neither did the animals that were lying with him. As she got close enough to see details, she saw blood. She began to scream as she threw down the lunch and ran as fast as she could to his side. When she realized that he was dead, she swooned and lay on the ground for some time unconscious. When she awoke, it was not a nightmare, but actually Abel lying there on the ground stiff and cold. She got to her wobbly legs and ran for Adam as fast as she could. She knew that he would be working his mines, so she went in that direction, almost exhausted when she finally arrived.

"Oh, Father, Abel is dead," she cried as she fell into his sweaty arms.

"What do you mean, he's dead? He can't be dead," Adam tried to reassure her. He had seen a few dead animals, so he knew what she meant.

"He's been killed. He's been beaten," screamed the distraught daughter.

Adam knew at once what had happened. He carried Lela to his house where Eve received the news almost as badly as Lela. She leaned into a corner of the wall, pounding it as she shrieked. They were not accustomed to death, and didn't know how to handle it. Eve became rational enough to stagger along behind Adam as he carried Lela to the place where Abel lay. There were no animals or birds about his body, and even insects had not adapted to dead things, so Abel's body was unmolested. When Eve and Lela saw it, they both began to scream as they fell to their knees, and rocked back and forth. Adam, too, lifted up his voice and wept. For hours they went on; they cast dust into the air above their heads, and tore their clothes in anguish. Eve cried that it was her fault because she had disobeyed God first, and Adam swore that h would kill Cain. The bloody mattock lying near the body was testimony enough that Cain had committed the devilish crime.

It was almost evening when the trio dried up, and then they began to wonder what to do with Abel's remains. Eve wanted to take the cadaver to her house, and keep it on a table in the living room. But Adam solved the dilemma by remembering that God told him that he was taken out of the soil.

"God made me from the soil," he said, "and back to the soil we must go. God told me that I must return to the soil, and so must Abel. We must leave him here on the ground, and allow him to go back to the soil."

It was dark when the three left the site of death. Lela felt uneasy, and wanted to go with Eve. Adam picked up the mattock before he left, determined to use it on Cain. Lela visited the place every day for two or three days, but then the body of Abel began to turn dark, and mummify. She could no longer bear to see him. She told her father of this, and he thought much about it. At last, went out to the place, and covered the body with earth and stones. This made Lela feel a little better when she went to the spot, and began putting flowers on the grave.

Cain fled from the scene of his crime straight to his house to see Dinah, but he had a terrible foreboding about what God would do in response to the crime. It hadn't been written yet, but somehow Cain knew it was a fact that you can be sure your sins will find you out, and God would not look lightly upon the death of his prophet, or any living soul. Cain didn't have long to wait. That very afternoon while he was in the field,

"And the LORD said unto Cain, Where is Abel thy brother? And he said, I know not: Am I my brother's keeper? [10]And he said, What hast thou done? the voice of thy brother's blood crith unto me from the ground. [11]And now art thou cursed from the earth, which hath opened her mouth to receive thy brother's blood from thy hand; [12] When thou tillest the ground, it shall not henceforth yield unto thee her strength; a fugitive and a vagabond shalt thou be in the earth". (Genesis 4).

God knew where Abel was – useless to lie about it – Abel was dead, his body cold yonder in the field of brutality. Now, we wonder why God did not strike Cain dead on the spot. He had the power and authority.

He killed everybody on Earth sixteen hundred years later because they were so violent.

"(For until the law sin was in the world: but sin is not imputed when there is no law. [14]Nevertheless death reigned from Adam to Moses, even over them that had not sinned after the similitude of Adam's transgression, who is the figure of him that was to come." (Romans 5)

God wouldn't kill Cain; but He would make his life so miserable that he would wish He had. Cain was cursed from the earth; he could no longer raise the tasty things he had raised from the earth, and now he would be a fugitive and a vagabond. Already his father was planning to kill him.

"And Cain said unto the LORD, My punishment is greater than I can bear. [14] Behold, thou hast driven me out this day from the face of the earth; and from thy face shall I be hid; and I shall be a fugitive and a vagabond in the earth; and it shall come to pass, that every one that findeth me shall slay me."

How many people have said, "My punishment is greater than I can bear?" Everybody that goes to Hell will say that. Cain stood before an angry, offended God, and God showed no mercy because there was no repentance. Cain was in a rage now because of God's judgment. He trembled with fear and trepidation. He feared Adam even more than he feared God.

"And the LORD said unto him, Therefore whosoever slayeth Cain, vengeance shall be taken on him sevenfold. And the LORD set a mark upon Cain, lest any finding him should kill him.

After the LORD finished with Cain, he lay for a long time wondering what he should do. He expected to see his father come out of the thicket any minute with the mattock, and blood in his eye. He got up, finally realizing that he would have to leave that part of the world. He had no idea how big the earth was, or which direction would be safest, he just knew that he would have to go. He couldn't fight his own father. He certainly could never see his parents again. For the first time, he felt a pang of sorrow as he thought of never seeing his mother again. His sorrow was for his plight. He loved his mother, in his own brutish way, but she was a thing of the past now.

Dinah was horrified when she heard the news. "Just pack up and leave our home and all we have?" For the first time, Dinah questioned her husband. "Where will we go and what will we do? You don't know what's over those hills. What if we encounter unknown animals or birds that will eat us. You don't even know what we'll eat!" She screamed at him.

"Shut up, Woman, and get your things together, I'm leaving here with you in a few minutes. We don't have time to waste." Cain retorted.

Dinah became hysterical; Cain slapped her, and shook her. He began gathering up things he wanted, and threw them on a sheepskin. They would have to travel light, because he didn't know how far they would have to flee.

Cain went off to Nod with Dinah following, crying as she went. In Nod he built a city with a palisade around it, and named it after his first born son, Enoch. A great civilization sprang from him, which was wiped out to the last infant in the great flood in Noah's day sixteen hundred years later. All because he would not obey God, not because he did not believe in God, but because he would not trust God for His blessings. He thought his works were good enough to please God, make him equal with God, but without faith, it is impossible to please God. (Hebrews 11:6)

HOW TO PREPARE TO GO TO HEAVEN

Romans 3

10. *As it is written, There is none righteous, no, not one:*

11. *There is none that understandeth, there is none that seeketh after God.*

12. *They are all gone out of the way, they are together become unprofitable; there is none that doeth good, no, not one.*

21. *But now the righteousness of God without the law is manifested, being witnessed by the law and the prophets;*

22. *Even the righteousness of God which is by faith of Jesus Christ unto all and upon all them that believe: for there is no difference:*

23. *For all have sinned, and come short of the glory of God;*

Romans 10

8. *But what saith it? The word is nigh thee, even in thy mouth, and in thy heart: that is, the word of faith, which we preach;*

9. *That if thou shalt confess with thy mouth the Lord Jesus, and shalt believe in thine heart that God hath raised him from the dead, thou shalt be saved.*

10. *For with the heart man believeth unto righteousness; and with the mouth confession is made unto salvation.*

11. *For the scripture saith, Whosoever believeth on him shall not be ashamed.*

12. *For there is no difference between the Jew and the Greek: for the same Lord over all is rich unto all that call upon him.*

13. *For whosoever shall call upon the name of the Lord shall be saved.*

AFTERGLOW

Does this little story have a point or a purpose, someone may ask. This story is small, but it carries eternal truths. No human can save himself from himself. It tells the ancient story of the first man who was ever born – a man who would rather burn than obey his Creator. Why do sinners so fear their Redeemer? Cain <u>knew</u> that God exists. He talked with Him: saw His works. Cain made a conscious decision to reject God's sovereignty. He demonstrated that he would rather be lost forever than to obey God. He would have done anything to please God, except obey Him. Cain insisted on serving God his way rather than God's way.

No man can save himself. No person can save us. No institution can save us. Though the sinner give everything he owns to the poor, it avails nothing. The rich man is too poor to buy salvation. The doctor is too dumb to save himself. The lawyer is too unlearned. The athlete is too weak. The farmer doesn't have enough land. All the rest of us fall short in one way or other. Icons and rituals are repulsive to God.

People reject God for two reasons mainly: 1. They know that God demands certain moral restraints in His children. 2. They are determined that no one will rule over them.

To go to Heaven, put all your faith and trust in the Lord Jesus Christ. Rest in Him.